SPEAK UP, STAND OUT AND SHINE

Speak Powerfully in Any Situation

Regina Huber

Speak up, Stand out and Shine – Speak Powerfully in Any Situation by Regina Huber

Published by Regina Huber

www.transformyourperformance.com

© 2016 Regina Huber.

First Edition

ISBN: 978-0-9889212-2-1

Cover by PixelStudio

Disclaimer:
I am not a psychologist. This book and the content provided herein are tools I have developed or adapted based on my background in Transformational Leadership Coaching, Human Resources, Training & Talent Development, Career Management, Diversity & Inclusion, Entrepreneurship, Holistic Healing & Wellness Consulting, Studies of the Human Mind, Dance, and Multi-Cultural Environments. The Reader is aware that this book is in no way to be construed as psychological counseling.

CONTENTS

Dedication

I dedicate this book to my beloved family, who always stand by my side even when they are far away: my parents Regina and Franz, my brothers Franz and Anton, my sisters Rosmarie and Martina, and my nephews Felix, Tobias and Moritz.

Acknowledgements

Among my many friends on all continents, special thanks go to Beatrix Heider, Marianne Lauber, Manuela Batchanzi, Daniel Martínez, Julia Relinghaus, Ana María Puértolas, Miriam Gualda, Ahmyna Haydd, Sabrina Ortiz, Chris Larose, Susan Davis, Ibrahima Sow, Vicky Roig, Liz Bull, Susan Gala, Gil Quintana, Christine and Jean-Manuel Izaret, Mary Anne Holliday, Julia Andrés, Cindy Ashton, Franc D'Ambrosio and Mireille Potter, who have supported me unconditionally during challenging moments of my life.

Thanks to all my soul mates for helping me grow.

Thank you, Chris Larose, for sweetening the last few years with nights of blissful dancing.

Thank you, Susan Davis, Susan Gala, Mary Anne Holliday and Lisa Jendza for being my test readers and providing valued feedback.

Thank you, Natasha Reid, for inspiring me to start writing, and to anyone who ever believed in me.

Warning:

Applying the techniques in this book may open your mind,
raise your confidence, enhance your visibility and increase your
success!

INTRODUCTION

This book was written for anyone who knows they have a message to share and wants to present it more powerfully. It was written for you if you are

- an employee aspiring to be a leader in your organization,
- a business owner who wants to get the word out about your products and services,
- an aspiring thought leader with an important message that needs to get out to the world,
- a corporate leader who wants to show up more powerfully in presentations or meetings,
- an activist looking to contribute to positive social change,
- a consultant seeking to deliver more engaging client presentations,
- looking to distinguish yourself as an expert by making more meaningful contributions in meetings,
- an instructor or training facilitator looking to be more impactful in your teachings, whether online or offline,
- interviewing for a job,

- a coach seeking for ways to publicly differentiate yourself as the unique professional you are,
- a scientist or inventor burning to personally communicate your latest findings,
- someone with a story that needs to be told to inspire others,
- an entrepreneur preparing to pitch to a group of investors,
- an attorney striving to demonstrate a persuasive presence in court,
- on a mission to share your passion with a larger audience,
- planning for a radio or TV appearance,
- considering taking on speaking so you can play bigger than you have so far.

If this is you, but you are somehow intimidated by the idea of putting yourself out there, then this is the book for you. This book will provide you with techniques that make speaking up in meetings, in front of a room or from a stage less daunting. It equips you with tools that can help you come across as more authentic and confident, and to connect with your audience on a deeper level. Speaking is key to leadership and self-leadership. It is a way to play bigger than you have so far.

Live Your Speaking Vision

Most people know that leadership is not tied to a specific position; good leadership doesn't come to someone simply because of a new job title. Leadership is an attitude combined with certain skills. Ultimately though, it doesn't matter how magnificent you are as a leader unless you move into the spotlight. As long as you don't speak up and stand out, you won't be able to inspire anyone with your leadership.

In order to inspire others, a powerful leader must be able to step in front of an audience, big or small, and speak confidently, intelligently and passionately. We must be able to move through our fear and have a compelling presence to engage our audience, whatever that audience may be: your team, a client, a room filled with prospective clients. We need to speak to inspire so we're not only heard but remembered. We need to touch people's lives with our message. That's how great leaders succeed every day.

Speaking up and standing out as a leader in any situation is not an easy task. It can be scary, challenging, overwhelming. The focus of this book is to provide you with the tools to help you face and manage your fears, turn your anxiety into excitement, and find the fun and joy in sharing your ideas and message. While a small portion of stage fright can be helpful to connect with your audience on a deeper level or make you sound more interesting, when the butterflies in your stomach go crazy on stage, you will need some effective tools to control them and calm down so you can focus on your topic and audience, rather than your nerves. Those tools are found throughout the rest of this book.

A message unused is a useless message. You have an important message to share. It needs to get out. And in order to make this happen, you have to expand your reach. So now is the time to take action! It's time to get aligned with your magnificence, to write a new script for your speaking career! It's time to speak up with confidence and monetize your skills!

I decided to write this book to help you find your magnetic speaking power and your confident presence, because I want you to capture all your opportunities to get your value and your message out to the world. Once you find that speaking power and confidence, you will be able to reach and inspire more people with your unique words and wisdom.

My Story

I wish I'd had these tools when I was in corporate. I often had to present unpopular news to my team, deliver training sessions, or present projects to the local Vice Presidents, without any speaking training or being able to practice frequently in real life situations. When I was called upon to do these things, I would get nervous and want to hide behind my desk. My heart would race, my face would flush, and I would get frazzled. I would want it to be over as fast as possible, so I would talk too fast and stumble over my own words, especially when people reacted with resistance or asked challenging questions. These leadership moments would have been so much easier had I applied the tools in this book. Now, I use these tools for every speaking engagement and business meeting I attend. They have made a huge difference in my confidence and presence on stage, which has led to greater success.

We write the book we need to read. We teach what we need to learn the most. Why? Well, if we had always done it naturally and we had known all the answers right from the start, we would never have had to figure it out, and we wouldn't have anything to teach or write about. How could I show you how to get from A to B if I never walked on that path myself, if I had never moved through this kind of transformation? But I have. And I want you to undergo that transformation too, and see the changes it will make in your life and the lives of those around you.

After I left the corporate world, I moved to Latin America and took a long break from speaking and teaching … eight years! When I came back to the United States, I wanted nothing to do with speaking. Except, I started networking and pitching my new business idea, and you need good speaking skills and a confident presence to do that. After eight years away from speaking, not only did I have a lot of catching up to do, but I knew I couldn't afford freaking out about speaking, especially when I wanted to be a business owner. If I wanted people to listen to me and to pay attention to my business offerings, I had to find a way to go from freaking out to freaking amazing. I created these tools to overcome the freak-out sessions and propel me to success. Years later, I have tested these tools, not only on myself countless times, but with numerous clients as well. I want to make these techniques available to you. I truly hope you will find them equally helpful as you build your speaker confidence and lead out in your area of expertise.

So, are you ready to go from freaking out to freaking amazing? If so, read on!

If you're like most people, you're probably somewhere in-between these two extremes of freaking out or being freaking amazing. Regardless of where you are, the best moment to start anything new is NOW!

The following chapters will show you the steps I take and the specific exercises and tools I use to prepare for speaking gigs: from preparing your mind to be a powerful speaker, to exercises you can do to overcome stage fright while actually on stage or in a meeting. You are already competent. Your competence needs confidence and training to overcome self-doubt, monotony and negative energy. This book offers you powerful tools to help you override momentary insecurity and nervousness, which surround fully embracing your best speaker self. They allow you to enhance your speaking presence, and step into the limelight with confidence every time you apply them.

Let's get started!

Exercise 1: Costs of Opportunity Lost

Before we dive into specific techniques, let's look at the opportunity costs to staying quiet. Go get a piece of paper and write down this question: "What is it costing me to keep quiet?" Before you start writing, close your eyes and think about it. Really think about it. Now, write down the answers that come. List everything that comes to mind. Are you losing money? Clients? Friendships? Are you missing out on living your purpose or supporting the causes that are close to your heart?

Now, look at what you wrote. We're going to turn it around and rephrase those statements positively, so we can see possible benefits from speaking up. For example, "I miss out on clients" could be turned around to, "I gain clients." Take a few minutes to rephrase each opportunity cost you listed.

Once that is complete, ask yourself these questions: What could you achieve if you put yourself in front of your ideal audience? What difference you could make? How many lives could you touch? How would your business change? How much more money could you be making?

When you've answered those, pick the top three reasons you *should* get out there and speak. Evaluate these three reasons: On a scale of 0 to 10, how much do they mean to you? How important are they? Consider each reason you listed to get out there and speak. If your answer is 0-5 for all three reasons, pass this book on to a friend who could benefit from it. If at least one of these reasons is anywhere above 5, read on!

Exercise 2: Create a Speaker's Board

Have you ever made a vision board? If not, I suggest you do. However, today I want you to create a Speaker's Board.

You can do this in PowerPoint or on paper. I like PowerPoint because I don't have a stack of magazines that I can use for images, and I can easily adapt it over time but it's really up to you. If you choose PowerPoint, make sure to print your board after creating it. Here's how I suggest doing this:

Put a picture of yourself in the middle of the page. If you have a picture of yourself speaking, use that photo. Draw dialog bubbles around or above the picture, and write one of your key messages in each bubble. Search for images with audiences on the internet (or in your magazines) and paste them on your slide.

Finally, add the names of specific events or audiences to the dialog bubbles with your key messages; if you have certain dates in mind, write them next to the events. You can always put a simple calendar in one corner of the board where you mark your important meetings, speaking, and presentation dates. There are more opportunities that you may think. Visit www.transformyourperformance.com/speaking-opportunities to see my *List of Speaking Opportunities to* get inspired.

Once completed, use your speaker's board as a visualization tool: See yourself as a powerful, influential leader, speaker and presenter who inspires others to take action from the stage or in front of a room. Envision yourself in this role every single day first thing in the morning. Allow it to inspire you to fill in the gaps in your speaking calendar. Look for opportunities online, at networking events. Call your contacts. Find out where your ideal audience and clients hang out, and apply to speak at those places. Research associations, clubs, and conferences. Find events related to your message, or even events that may allow out-of-category speakers in, as long as your topic benefits their audience. Book it now and prepare later! If you are in corporate, volunteer to deliver presentations on relevant topics when opportunities arise and proactively create your own opportunities. Speaking is a way to distinguish yourself as an expert, cut yourself away from your peers, and gain visibility. Trust that you can do it and use the tools in this book to get yourself there.

You are now ready for the empowering tools I will share with you in the following chapters. In Part I, we will cover some basic concepts and exercises that allow you to step into your best speaker self. Part II will teach techniques that allow you to optimally prepare during the week before your important event, while Part III, will discuss ways to manage your nerves the day and night before the event. Part IV teaches you ways to brace yourself for your event the day of. In Part V, I'll give you some tips to successfully navigate through the event itself so you can more easily access the full range of your inner resources and deliver a masterful presentation. The final part (Part VI) will touch on some key aspects to work on after the event to improve future performance.

Grab a notebook or piece of paper and start a list of your preferred tools. As you come upon exercises that help and resonate with you, take note of them. Integrate them into your pre-speaking and pre-meeting routine. Complete the list as you continue reading and experimenting with the exercises I teach throughout this book.

Read on and enjoy the experience of speaking powerfully in any situation!

PART I:
ESSENTIAL PREPARATIONS

This part introduces you to some fundamental concepts like distinctive uniqueness, authenticity and vulnerability, which help you transform into a powerful speaker, presenter and negotiation partner.

Chapter 1

STEP INTO YOUR BEST SPEAKER SELF

Most people don't book speaking gigs just for the fun of it (even if it actually *can* be fun). Most people are motivated to speak to make a lasting impression on people. You want them to remember you, talk about you, and buy from you, whether the product you sell is a service or an idea. So what does it take to be noticeable, memorable, remarkable, distinctive, unforgettable? It's not only about a great message (I'm assuming you have that). After you have your basic speaking skills under your belt, I believe there are three key elements needed to raise you to stardom as a speaker: uniqueness, authenticity and vulnerability.

Discover Your Distinctive Uniqueness

Distinctive Uniqueness is one of my favorite things to teach my clients. Put simply, your distinctive uniqueness is the expression of your unique qualities. These could be talents, skills, personality traits, qualifications, your unique story, ideas, perspectives, gestures, your winning smile, and anything else that defines who you are, why you do what you do, and how you present yourself. For the sake of your success, focus on those unique assets that are most beneficial to others' perceptions of you and are aligned with your message and what you stand for.

Whether we like it or not, every person sees us in a unique light. We are judged and branded from the moment someone sees us for the first time. The best way to influence this initial judgment is to have a say in what they see. Ultimately, how others see us depends on how we see ourselves. The way we can influence their judgments of us is by acknowledging our uniqueness. Acknowledging our uniqueness is twofold: First, it is simply getting clear on what distinguishes us from other people who have similar offerings. Second it is defining how we see ourselves.

Have you ever wondered why some people get more attention than others, and attract more business and more clients? Why does it seem everyone wants to attend their events? Why did they get the promotion you wanted? There are probably several reasons for this attention, but one thing is certain: These people stand out from the crowd. They distinguish themselves from others in some way. They have identified their own uniqueness and they are not afraid to show it in their appearance, their outfit, their branding, their business cards, their style, the way they hold themselves, etc. Simply put, they embrace their distinctive uniqueness and let it shine. They are *not ordinary*. They are *extra-ordinary* in some way, and they know they are.

Do you know *you are* extraordinary? Because of our distinctive uniqueness, we are all capable of being extraordinary, if we want to be.
You. Are. *Extraordinary*.
Do you believe it?

Maybe you need some more convincing. Let's find out what makes you distinct, unique and extraordinary.

Exercise 3: Show Me Your Unique Assets
What makes you unique? Grab a pen and paper and make a list of 50 things that make you unique. Without thinking specifically of

your business or career, write down anything that's special or unique about you, or anything about yourself that makes you stand out. How are you different? Don't only think about the obvious! Think outside the box. Go beyond professional traits and skills and list personal qualities as well. Often times we think the more personal features are not important. But if you're a speaker, we want to connect with your *person*. People connect with people. So make your list of your strengths, abilities, talents, gifts, skills, personality traits, physical features, accomplishments, qualifications, style, etc. Include anything that makes you special. I call these qualities your "unique assets" because some of them are worth gold. Together, these qualities and assets work together to become your unique appeal to those around you.

Having trouble coming up with your list? Send out a brief anonymous online survey to a number of friends and ask them what three qualities come to mind when they think of you. Or directly ask them what they think is unique about you. This will give you insights about how people see your uniqueness in every day and professional life.

Now we're going to create your Distinctive Uniqueness Profile. This is done by taking your list of unique assets and dividing it up into specific areas or roles where you want to demonstrate your uniqueness. Some roles include team leader, mother, brother, or boss. List those roles at the top of a piece of paper, then allocate your individual unique assets to the roles they support. You will find that many are relevant for several or all the roles you play in your life. They all play into each other. This is proof of the enormous value of your distinctive uniqueness.

Now you have two lists. Using either one, circle the ten assets that will be most beneficial to magnify in order to distinguish yourself as an expert or leader in your job or in your field. Reflect on how you can magnify these qualities in your work and in your marketing. As a speaker, how can you turn them into your "unique appeal?" Write down some of the ideas so you can begin implementing them today.

This exercise helps us recognize how unique we really are. It makes perfect sense that we are meant to be unique because each of us has a singular role in the bigger scheme. Your personal strengths, talents and skills complement those of the people around you. When you deeply understand your distinctive uniqueness, you align with your brilliance. Remember, how others see us depends on how we see ourselves. The more clearly we see our own, unique value, the more others will be able to see it, too. This is when we really start to become that powerful, engaging and motivational speaker in the business meeting, the management meeting, or on the public stage.

Your Story Is Your Gem

Another unique asset is your story. No one else on this entire planet has the same story as you. You may have heard this before: People forget what you said, but they recall how you made them feel. Others respect us for our knowledge and our expertise, but they connect with us emotionally. They connect emotionally through your story.

Everyone has a story. What's yours? I am sure you have many stories worth telling. Which of them is the one that relates to why you're speaking to this crowd, to why you do what you do, to why you are who you are these days, to why you want to share this message?

There's a whole science around storytelling. There are experts who specialize in helping speakers, politicians, and entrepreneurs craft their stories. Why? Because your story is so critically important. It's what ties you in with your audience on a deep level. It's what creates rapport. And often times your story is actually what qualifies you to speak about a specific topic or work in a specific field. Your story is what shows others that you are the expert and that you understand their challenges, that you *get* them, even if you're still figuring some details out yourself on your path to mastery.

If I had been born as a confident, power-conscious person with a compelling presence, I wouldn't be able to understand others who are struggling in this area. I know what it feels like to be shy. I get it. I was just like that.

If you're not clear on your story (yet), pause here and take a moment to reflect on what's a significant event in your life that marked you deeply. How does it relate to what you do? What caused you to choose your profession, your job, your business? There are probably several relevant events. Jot down your ideas, then choose the most compelling one and write down the story around it. Keep refining it as you test it with different audiences. In the beginning, we tend to get into too much detail as we travel back in time and get caught up in our past, but over time your story will become more captivating, and you will learn to easily adapt it to a given topic. It will be fascinating to see how people immediately relate to you in a different way once they hear it.

Since we've significantly boosted your self-esteem with your magnificent distinctive uniqueness and by motivating you to tell a story with you as the main character, you may feel like pulling back because you are afraid of being prideful. Let me address this briefly.

Humility and What It Really Means
Most of us were brought up to be humble. This is especially true for women. Humility is frequently the excuse to live mediocre lives below our potential; it's an excuse to blend in and stay small rather than stand out. We don't step up to leadership roles because who are *we* to be leaders? We stay invisible, because standing out from the crowd would be arrogant. We don't talk about our accomplishments, because bragging is prideful. It's interesting how the one thing we do brag about is how humble we are.

Embracing our distinctive uniqueness and shining like a star isn't humble, is it?

Actually, it *is*.

I like telling my clients two things about humility, "Playing big is the new humble," and, "Standing out is the new humble." I even made a short video for you about this view of humility, which you can view on YouTube with the title *Playing Big Is the New Humble*.

Here's the thing: True humility is about stepping up to our full potential; it's recognizing that we have been given talents and abilities and using them the way they were intended. It's about working up the courage to show our uniqueness so the world can benefit from our unique talents and skills, whether that's in corporate or whether we offer our products and services to our clients directly as business owners. Humility is showing gratitude in our successes, and success will inevitably come when we embrace our strengths and let them shine.

So let's move away from false humility, which says I have to hide who I am and the greatness inside of me! Instead, let's move towards this belief: "It is my responsibility to show my authentic, distinctive uniqueness to those around me so I can contribute to this world what I came here to do." The world needs you and your contribution! It's both your birthright and your responsibility to live the life you are meant to live and to share the message you are here to share. You owe it to yourself. I know that your true self has high expectations for you. This is the part of you which is constantly nudging you to speak your truth because it's an important aspect of living your purpose. Your true self wants you to play big and speak loud and clear so more people can hear you, so you can make a bigger difference, so you can change more lives and play your part in the overall scheme of things. So you can become more of who you are. Being unique is about living your purpose. We were created as unique human beings with a unique purpose, so we could contribute our gifts to the world and complement each other as individual pieces of the overall puzzle. Humility is accepting this responsibility, transcending our perceived limitations, and living our unique greatness to the benefit of those around us.

Embrace Your Uniqueness

There's another important aspect to our unique assets: When we focus on our unique strengths instead of our weaknesses, this automatically increases our self-esteem and raises our confidence. When we start from what we do well, what we are good at, it's much easier to feel good about ourselves and our potential. We are not supposed to be good at *everything*! The beauty of uniqueness is that we human beings complement each other with our unique strengths (and ideally we'd also compliment each other for them). It's why different people do different things, have different jobs, and own different businesses. Once you fully acknowledge your strongest strengths, your unique assets, and your potential, you are empowered to act on them and doing so compensates for your shortcomings more easily. What we focus on expands. When you focus on your talents, skills, and accomplishments, their energy expands and they will be magnified, while your weaknesses will diminish.

Not *everybody* will like you, and that's ok. However, when you show your authentic power and uniqueness, some people will LOVE you! The ones who love you are your ideal clients and fans. They will advocate for you and support you. Acknowledging this fact will save you from having to deal with prospects that are not your ideal clients anyway. Let's say you go into a department store, and there are 20 equal dresses, same cut, same size, same color. How do you know which one to choose? Now imagine that you walk into a boutique and you're looking for an elegant, yet trendy outfit for a special occasion. You see a beautiful piece that seems like it was made for you! You have never seen anything like it. It's just perfect for your body type, your style, and this specific occasion. And you love its unique print. This piece has your name written all over it. Would you rather buy the boring dress on a rack and risk that someone else could be wearing the same dress at a networking event or buy the one-of-a-kind gown and stand out? Let's put it another way: As a business owner or speaker, would you rather *be* that boring dress on a rack or the one-of-a-kind gown? Would you rather be the compact car or the Lamborghini? Don't get lost in sameness and conformity. Let your individuality shine! It's what we want to see.

So who are *you* and what do you bring to the table? It's worth getting some clarity around this. Remember, when you truly see your uniqueness, others will be able to see it, too

Authenticity Creates Trust

Now that we are comfortable with who we are and the talents and abilities we bring to the table, we need to be authentic and genuine in our relationships and conversations. Authenticity is "the quality of being real or true," according to Cambridge Dictionary.[1] I believe authenticity is also about acting in accordance with your highest values, expressing your truth and living up to your personal standards.

Many people talk about authenticity these days, and there's a good reason for doing so: An authentic person is a person who we will want to be around and follow. We feel we can trust them and the message they share. Being truly authentic requires courage and vulnerability. You have to take down the walls between you and your audience and really connect heart to heart.

Think about how trust is built: You meet someone, get to know them through conversations and interactions over time, and slowly trust is built. On stage, in a business meeting, or on a sales call, the time to build that trust is taken away; that's why authenticity is so important. When you are truly being you, when you come across as transparent and real, you allow others to connect to you more quickly, which builds the trust you need to close a deal, make a sale, or simply impact your team.

One of the ways to be authentic is through genuine smiling. A smile signals friendliness and good intention, but only as long as it's a real, heartfelt smile. People feel it when your smile is fake. A fake smile actually detracts from your credibility. For people who talk from their hearts, smiling at the right time of their talks comes naturally. They don't have to think about it, but their audience will notice it. The audience will take subsequent action when they can trust you because of your authenticity.

Another way to be authentic is by being yourself in everything you say and do. Don't try to be someone else. Everyone else is already taken! There are currently about 7.3 billion people on this planet, and none of them has your DNA, no one has your fingerprint,

---

[1] *Cambridge Dictionary, s.v.* "Authenticity," accessed September 5, 2016, http://dictionary.cambridge.org/us/dictionary/english/authenticity.

no one has your iris.[2] There is only one *you* on this Earth. You are unmatched. As Dr. Seuss claims, "There is no one alive who is you-er than you!"[3] Remember, you were created as a uniquely brilliant and complete being, perfect in who you are in every moment with the option to grow beyond your current level at any given time. You came here with your own very unique and special gifts, talents, purposes, and style. The world needs exactly *you*, because the other people are already doing their own stuff. What if you could be more successful by sharing who you truly are? By you being *you*? By you sharing *you* with those who need a "piece" of *you*: *your* message, *your* contribution, or *your* support? That's the power of authenticity, of being YOU instead of trying to be someone else.

People often pull away from authenticity because it is too vulnerable and shows imperfections. Too many people suffer from a need to be perfect, but perfectionism is counterproductive: It can stop us from doing important things like speaking up in the first place. Always remember, perfection in all you do is an illusion. It can't be obtained by any one! Instead, declare that you are perfectly imperfect and good enough as you are and move forward! We've learned in so many ways that we are not good enough. It's time to un-learn that! Instead of continuing on the limiting wavelength of perfectionism, strive for showing your uniqueness so people notice you and you cannot be ignored any longer.

It takes guts to be yourself. I'm sure you have them. Dare to be you!

Vulnerability Is the New Strong
Authenticity requires a deep level of vulnerability, because you're dropping walls and letting people see you for who you are, the good *and* the bad. I see vulnerability as the willingness to show others who you truly are, without putting on a mask or playing a role. Vulnerability is often considered a weakness, but it's really a place from which you can feel joy, love, empathy, and strength. It's a place

---

[2] U.S. Department of Commerce, "Population Clock", accessed September 5, 2016, http://www.census.gov/.
[3] Dr. Seuss, *Happy Birthday to You!* (New York: Random House, 1959)

from where we build human ties. The truth is, if I build armor around myself it's much harder to make a meaningful connection with you, however short- or long-lived it may be. Vulnerability is a way to take down that armor and connect us together. Vulnerability can be a source of power for you, especially as you stand out and speak up.

As previously discussed, we often suffer from a need to be perfect or simply appear perfect. However, perfectionism is illusionary. It is unattainable. Stop striving for perfection and start embracing your distinctive uniqueness and authentic personality. We've learned in so many ways that we are not good enough just as we are, but this is not true. It's time to un-learn that lie! We must realize that we are absolutely good enough and even better than we can comprehend. Instead of continuing on the limiting wavelength of perfectionism, strive for showing your uniqueness, authenticity and be vulnerable with those around you. People will notice you and start to take action on what you say.

Vulnerability is about showing your imperfections and mistakes. Imperfections make you more likeable; mistakes deepen your relationship with your audience. Both can even help you increase your stage presence. It doesn't matter that you have flaws; it's all about how you react to your own mistakes and imperfections, both in the moment they happen and when discussing them in conversation or on stage. This makes you more vulnerable and therefore more human and more relatable than when you are overly polished. While vulnerability does require courage, it also gives you power and it sets you apart from those around you.

Vulnerability requires that you face your fear of being exposed as being human and less-than-perfect and move through that fear with grace and dignity. Being vulnerable can accelerate our growth, as we openly face our current shortcomings so we can transcend them. Moving to our next level frequently feels like stepping into the unknown and outside our comfort zone. Fear of the unknown often follows stepping outside our comfort zone; this fear is simply a negative projection into the future, which has been created by your own mind. Often times it's an irrational fear that lacks any substance and purpose.

The next chapter will explain why fear exists and when it does and does not serve. It will also explain why we often feel fear, even extreme fear, when there's no life-threatening risk, like in public speaking.

Chapter 2

BREAK FREE FROM THE CHAINS OF FEAR

Many people stay quiet, turn down speaking gigs, and miss out on sales opportunities because they are afraid. While fear has its place in the world, we often let it rule our lives and hold us back from doing those things which will bring us the most happiness and fulfillment in life.

When Fear Is Good

Fear is not a bad thing. Fear can literally save your life; it keeps you safe and alive. It causes you to refrain from jumping down a precipice, from crossing the street when a truck is passing, or from running into the arms of a bear or the jaws of a lion.

Think of a scary or life-threatening experience from your past: did fear protect you by putting you on auto-pilot to do something that you wouldn't usually do or accomplish something you normally could not have accomplished? This happens because when our lives are threatened, our reptilian brain triggers a fight, flight, or freeze reaction. This is a protection mechanism, an automatic biological response that helps us cope with danger.

Fight, flight, and freeze are acute stress responses, which make total sense in life-threatening situations. The problem is, we also go into fight, flight, or freeze mode in other stressful situations where there's no real threat, such as public speaking.

When Fear Is Bad

Not all fear is good. A lot of fear we hold inside ourselves is actually bad fear. Bad fear stops us from taking action: action like applying for speaking gigs or putting ourselves and our work out there. In fact, for many people, this fear turns into torture when it comes to stepping in front of an audience. Often times, this fear or torture stems from a fear of rejection, and it is a horrible, limiting fear which will hold you back from success in whatever field you may be in.

Fear becomes a problem when it holds us back, when it stops us from playing big and putting ourselves out there, and ultimately from living our purpose or mission, from implementing our vision. Common types of fear in this context are: fear of public speaking (also called speech anxiety or glossophobia), fear of failure, fear of change, fear of the unknown, fear of rejection, fear of commitment, fear of conflict or conflicting opinions, etc.

If you have ever procrastinated picking up the phone to ask for a speaking opportunity, my guess is that you suffer from fear of rejection, as so many people do. You're either afraid that the person on the other end of the line might say, "No," or you're afraid that they might say, "Yes," and you actually have to do it! Even if the event host likes you, the audience might not like you, or there might be someone in the room who clearly doesn't wish you well. In any case, there is a risk that someone might reject you. We learned early on in life how painful it can be to get a "no."

I'm sure all of us at some point in our lives have been in a situation where we should have been given something we wanted but we didn't get it; or where we should have been selected for a sports team, for a promotion, or as a lover, but someone else was picked instead, right?

We've all been there! We all know what rejection feels like. Rejection hurts. It leaves very deep scars. In some cases, it can destroy our self-esteem. In most cases, rejection creates fear.

Fear of rejection is one of the most limiting emotions. It blocks you from truly connecting with your audience because you're afraid to be vulnerable with them. Your fear that they may say "no" to you or your message takes your focus away from the important content you want to share and from how you can connect with them on a deep level and points your focus inward. This distances you from the audience and makes you less credible. When you're not credible, they won't trust you and they won't listen to you. And they certainly won't buy from you, whether you're selling a product, a service, or an idea.

How else does fear of rejection affect our willingness to speak up? Often when we are rejected, we are traumatized. Trauma can cause us to build up fear in either our conscious or subconscious mind. When we have built up fear, especially buried in our subconscious mind, we sabotage our efforts to succeed without even realizing it. A past rejection can lead us to refrain from playing big and to miss out on our calling altogether.

Let me illustrate this with a very real, very personal experience. For the longest time, this connection between a past trauma and current fear did not occur to me. But one day, out of the blue, I remembered an important recurring childhood event, which traumatized me pretty deeply. Subsequently, I built up an enormous amount of fear in my subconscious mind. This fear sabotaged my ability to speak up for far too long.

As a child, I was always picked last for volleyball games at school. The best players were always chosen as team captains and had the privilege to choose the rest of the team. Since they wanted to win, they tried to get as many other great players onto their teams as possible. By now you may have guessed that I was not one of those great players. We'd all stand in a long line of kids, and the team captains would call out names: "Barbara," "Claudia," "Angela," … and with each name my heart sunk a bit deeper… until I was the only one left. – Because I wasn't good enough! I wasn't strong enough, I wasn't fast enough, I wasn't skilled enough! I just was not a sporting ace. While these thoughts may or may not have been entirely true, they were the beliefs I took upon myself at that time, simply because I was chosen last.

Over the years, I forgot about this experience, probably on purpose. Besides having more important things to think about, I didn't want to think about this experience. But when I started speaking, all of a sudden these images came back to me. I was again in a situation where I might be criticized for my skills and abilities, where I might not be good enough, and where I might be rejected. I realized that the simple fact of being chosen last for a volleyball game over 30 years in my past had created a fear of rejection that was sabotaging my success as a speaker and possibly as a business owner. For example, when it was my turn to pitch my business at a networking event, I'd get nervous about convincing my audience with the right words instead of focusing on connecting with the audience and speaking from my heart. I was afraid if I didn't say the right thing, the audience would reject my message all together. Eventually, I knew I needed to get over it.

How did I get over this debilitating fear? I learned about identifying limiting beliefs and fears and replacing them with positive, empowering emotions.

It's important to understand that over 95% of our behavior is driven by our subconscious (unconscious) mind, and only about 5% or less of our behavior is controlled by our conscious mind.[4] Our conscious mind thinks it is in control of the impact we have and the choices we make, but what's really in control is our subconscious programming.

Our subconscious mind is like a recorder: It records all our experiences, and as both studies and my work with my clients show,

---

[4] Marianne Szegedy-Maszak, "Mysteries of the Mind: Your Unconscious is making Your Every Day Decisions," accessed September 7, 2016, http://www.auburn.edu/~mitrege/ENGL2210/USNWR-mind.html.

it even records experiences of our ancestors, passed on to us in our genes.[5] We also continuously pick up "stuff" from the collective unconscious, the world that surrounds us, and other dimensions. Think of our subconscious as a computer program that has been filled up with our own experiences, our ancestors' experiences, and anything else we've absorbed energetically over our lifetime. This program constantly runs in the background and keeps us on auto-pilot, regardless of what we may consciously think we want.

Look at your results. Results are an indicator of your true subconscious beliefs. Have you ever repeated unhealthy patterns over and over, like attracting abusive relationships, perpetuating bad habits, procrastinating on revenue-generating tasks, etc.? We all have. And it's all because of the subconscious beliefs we may or may not realize we have, which are sabotaging our conscious efforts. There's good news and bad news about this. The bad news is these results will likely keep occurring unless you upgrade your "software" and get rid of the viruses. But here's the good news: You can change your programming! By doing what I did and identifying the limiting beliefs and emotions, and replacing them with positive, empowering thoughts and emotions, you can reprogram your subconscious mind to get the results you want. There are quite a few ways of doing this, some of which you can accomplish on your own and are listed as exercises included in this book. Other ways require the help of an expert because we often have some crazy subconscious beliefs that don't (and won't) make any sense to the conscious mind, and therefore the conscious mind cannot capture those beliefs by itself. For more information on how to reprogram your subconscious mind in a way that serves your sales goals and your success, you can contact me on my website www.transformyourperformance.com.

Let's return to fear of rejection. If you have had an experience like the one at school I described earlier, or any other experience where you felt rejected, your subconscious mind may have recorded that experience and taken on a limiting belief about risk and

---

[5] Linda Geddes, "Fear of Smell can be Passed Down Several Generations," *New Scientist,* December 1, 2013, https://www.newscientist.com/article/dn24677-fear-of-a-smell-can-be-passed-down-several-generations.

rejection. From then on when your subconscious sees any risk, like when you pick up the phone to ask for a speaking gig it immediately goes on alert: "Securityyyyyyyyyy!!!" it yells. Your subconscious is just doing its number one job (keeping you safe), so it keeps you from being hurt by causing you to procrastinate on signing up to speak in the first place. Or you get yourself around to make the call, but then you sabotage the opportunity by not being confident or assertive enough when applying for a spot. This is the way your subconscious mind is trying to protect you, to keep you safe from another risky experience. But what is it protecting you from exactly? Most often it's protecting you from your success! And is that really a protection? For most people, the answer to that question is a resounding, "NO!"

So then we have to ask ourselves: What's the real risk? What's the worst thing that can happen if I make that call? Get on stage? Speak up at a meeting? The worst thing that can happen is probably rejection of some sort, but you won't die! What if your audience actually likes you? That's always a possibility, too. But if you don't make the call, you're not even giving them a chance to say yes to you and to your message. Because of your fear, they won't be able to benefit from your inspiration, to improve their health, their love life or their professional success, or whatever your message may be. In short, your fear may inhibit their chance to change their lives for the better. Do you really want to deprive all these people from the precious gift and wisdom you have to share? I hope the answer to this question is "No" because you'd also deny yourself a fulfilled life of living your purpose and your dreams and making a difference in the unique way that's only available to you.

Simple Tools with Big Results
A former client of mine is a good example of the results we can achieve when we reframe limiting beliefs and fears. Shelley asked for an urgent coaching session with me one weekend in order to prepare for a presentation in front of her boss and a large and extremely demanding audience of prospective clients[6]. We briefly re-framed some of her concerns so she could leave her fear behind, and

---

[6] Name has been changed.

I taught her a number of tools to use before the presentation. After her big gig she called me saying her boss had been extremely pleased with her performance and she'd been able to convince the prospects of the benefits of their new product not only through the facts she presented, but also through her enthusiastic and authentic presentation style. Shelley easily managed to establish trust and connect with her audience in a way that made them well-disposed right from the start. Afterwards, she received raving feedback from her boss and co-workers who were present at the meeting. Reframing her beliefs made all of this possible.

It's important to note the beliefs she turned around before this presentation:

"My boss will be there and he will scrutinize every single word I say" turned into "What if this is an awesome opportunity to finally show my boss how powerful I am in the presence of prospects and clients?"

"I never spoke in front of such a large group, and there's just too much at stake!" became "This is a great opportunity to reach more people at the same time, and to show them our amazing new product. I am honored to be the one to present it to them."

She had the thought, "My boss must think very highly of me if he entrusts me with this important presentation." This last thought also inspired her to re-think her own impression about herself and she thought, "It seems that my boss sees me as more powerful than I see myself. Maybe there's something to it?" This breakthrough led to a whole new discussion of her self-image, which we worked on in a subsequent session. And it instantly sparked her courage.

Chapter 3

LET'S TALK COURAGE

So far, everything that we've talked about from speaking up to tackling limiting and self-sabotaging beliefs takes bravery and a whole lot of courage. It isn't easy facing an audience of hundreds of people, but it can be even scarier to face our subconscious and try to turn around sabotaging fears and beliefs. That's why courage is so essential to becoming the powerful speakers we need to be as leaders in our field of expertise.

The way I see it, there are three different types of courage we need to be successful: courage to be persistent, courage to try new things, and courage to leave behind what doesn't serve us.

Courage to Be Persistent

Let's start with the courage to be persistent. Yes, it requires courage to be persistent! It's much easier to give up when we don't immediately see results. We all experience setbacks in our lives. There is a saying that the most successful people are the ones who failed the most. Successful people call their failures lessons or stepping stones, which helps them move forward on their way to mastery and excellence. They allow themselves to "fail forward." We could say their failures become rehearsals for their success. They were courageous in their failures and persistent enough to continue forward. This led them to success when others failed.

Courage to Try New Things
Courageous persistence will only get you so far, especially if you keep doing what you've always done. To really change and step into your best speaker self, you need courage to try new things. Life is a game of trial and error. Life is about learning and growing and working up the courage to try something new in the midst of opposition, whether that opposition comes from inside your mind or from others around you. In order to make your contribution to this world, whatever your role or purpose may be, you may need to embrace other alternatives which may propel you to success and fulfilment. At times we think we have run out of alternatives, but this is never true. There is an abundance of options; we just have to open all our reception channels to perceive them so we can grasp the best ones. It takes courage to do this, especially if doing so is new or foreign.

Courage to Leave Behind What Doesn't Serve Us
Finding new ways and moving on to a new approach often requires courage to leave behind what doesn't serve us. We must detach from the things and relationships that do not serve our vision or goals anymore, especially negative influences. We must realize that while some people may stay with us for most of our lives, others have a short-term, temporary role, even if it is hard to part. We come into each other's lives to help one another grow and learn certain lessons. Sometimes we must make space in our heart and in our mind so we can let in new people and ideas. This can be a painful process and will take a LOT of courage.

This is also about leaving beliefs, thought patterns, and habits behind that don't serve us anymore – maybe some of them never did. For example, if your morning routine doesn't allow you a few minutes to meditate on how you want your day to go, thus creating a positive outlook, maybe it's time to change and let go of starting your day in a stressful way. Saying, "That's how we've always done it," doesn't make it better when it comes to limiting habits or patterns, and it's not a valid justification. Experiment with new approaches, new ways of doing things, and allow yourself to be surprised by a more positive outcome.

The following are some exercises where you can practice being courageous. In these exercises you will eliminate fears and limiting beliefs and free up new energy, which will take all three types of courage we've just discussed. Doing so will help you feel more liberated and powerful, two essential ingredients for speaking.

Exercise 4: Transforming Limiting Fear into Liberating Courage

To a large extent, we don't even consciously know what we believe. It's only when we dig deeper that we realize there is a gap between what we think we believe and what our behavior and results tell us about our beliefs. We may consciously think we want something or believe something, but our subconscious believes something different. Therefore, our results differ from those conscious beliefs and desires we think we hold. So let's look at your results: They are an indicator of your true subconscious beliefs. What results are you seeing in your life that aren't serving you?

Now let's tie that back to an underlying fear based on a past story. Take a moment to think about it. Discovering the event that brought this fear into your system is already a huge step towards deactivating its malicious effect on the actions you may or may not take. Look for situations related to your family, friends, school, dating, career, etc. Maybe ask yourself, "When have I been rejected in the past?" Then think about how this relates to your current life, to your business, to speaking. Is this incident causing the results you're seeing? What fear have you been carrying around since this incident? Name it.

Now ask yourself if this fear serves you in any way? Does it make you procrastinate? Does it block you from speaking in public, closing more business deals, making more money? Regardless of the fear, the truth is your life could be much better without it!

In order to let go of this fear, you will need to connect with it first. Rather than resisting it, invite the fear in and acknowledge it. Close your eyes and feel into the fear. Where in your body do you sense it creeping in? Does it have a specific density or color to it? Pay attention to the details.

Then thank the fear for its intention to protect you from rejection or disappointment, or whatever else it may be. Tell the fear that you see where it's coming from, but the reality is that it has been more limiting than protecting. Let the fear know that you will be ok without its protection and that you are perfectly able to take care of yourself. Then allow it to leave; let it go! Picture your fear moving out of your system and into an imaginary bubble. This could be a transparent soap bubble, a balloon, or any bubble of your choice. Finally, send the bubble with your fear out into the galaxy so it can be transmuted and transformed into neutral energy.

Now, picture that neutral energy you just created and watch it transform into courage. Bring this new courage energy all the way down in front of you. Use your hands to pull it down right in front of your chest. Holding your hands about eight to ten inches apart, palms facing each other, feel that courage energy between your hands. Play with the distance between your hands until you can literally feel the energy that's contained in the space between your hands. If you have trouble feeling the energy, push and pull a little or imagine a tennis ball going back and forth between your hands. This usually makes it easy to feel the energy quite intensely.

Once you can feel the energy between your hands, move your hands towards your heart and bring this courage energy into your chest with a big deep breath. Notice how you feel. Enjoy the powerful, liberating courage you just created for yourself and celebrate overcoming your fear!

Repeat this process every time fear creeps in, because it *will* continue to creep in even if it's likely to diminish over time. The truth is, I don't know anyone who is completely free of fear. What's critical is that we know how to manage our fear so we can function in the best way possible, especially in challenging situations.

Your mind generates a constant stream of thoughts, both positive and negative. Your thoughts determine your feelings, such as fear. You can't stop your thoughts, but you can turn them around. Instead of feeding negative, disempowering neural connections, what you want to do is interrupt them and replace them with positive, empowering pathways, which then evolve into positive neural patterns. The more positive neuro-circuits you build, the easier it will get to deal with fear quickly and effectively, which will make you a better public speaker. This exercise, repeated each time a fear comes up, will help you interrupt negative emotions and fear and replace them with the courage you want in your life.

Every time fear sneaks in, remind yourself of this: Fear is only a fantasy. It exists only in your mind. If you have created it, you can also un-create it, and re-create it into something that serves you better, like courage. Simple as that!

Taking the Power out of Traumatic Experiences

At a speaker training I attended not too long ago, we were asked to share our five-minute signature talk in front of the room. At the time, my signature talk was just a draft. Actually, it was more like a vague idea with a basic structure, as this was very much at the beginning of my speaking career.

I volunteered as one of the first speakers, mainly because I wanted it to get over with, and, surprisingly, I wasn't terribly nervous. I started speaking and got entangled in my own story; my story alone was going to fill the five minutes. I knew there was a lot to work on.

One of the coaches eventually interrupted me and said, "You are a hot mess." Then several coaches went on to pull my performance apart in front of the entire room, not accepting one single answer I provided to their questions. The result was that I felt awful for the rest of the event.

What was worse than feeling awful was that this event had been so traumatic that it threw me back several levels in my confidence as a speaker. When this trauma continued to impact me, I became acutely aware of its severity and origin and how it created an automatic trigger to feel like a "hot mess" every time I was in front of an audience, and especially in front of people who were in that circle. Because of this trigger, I knew it was time to cut the cords!

When I say it was time to cut the cords, I mean energetic cords. We are all energy and we are all connected through energy. This is unchangeable and how it is meant to be. However, as we establish a relationship with another person, we intensify our energetic attachment with them. It's as if we have a cord of energy connecting us together. That's what I refer to as "energetic cords."

As long as we are in a harmonious relationship with this person this attachment feels good, and the cords are filled with positive energy. But when a relationship becomes toxic or just doesn't serve us anymore, the cords may become filled with negative energy. If that's the case, it's time to cut the energetic cords and ties to that person to ensure this attachment doesn't adversely affect or limit us in any way going forward. How do you know if it's advisable to cut the cords? For example, a person may have disrespected or hurt you deeply, and although you are not seeing this person anymore, you feel like you can't get over it. Cutting energetic cords can help you get over it and free yourself up energetically for new, more nurturing relationships.

Exercise 5: Cutting Energetic Cords from Past Experiences

Picture the cords that connect you with the other person. If it was a romantic relationship, you may imagine these cords to go from heart to heart. If you're connected with the person through resentment, maybe the cords are going from brain to brain. Just be open and see what comes up when you visualize the cords. There is no right or wrong.

Now, imagine a gigantic pair of scissors and cut these cords in two. If scissors are not big or strong enough, use an imaginary axe and hack through the ties. While you are doing this, you may want to declare that you intend to maintain all positive connections that consist of unconditional love.

You may ask yourself if this really works. Just observe what it feels like when you finish. Your feelings will tell you the truth much more reliably than your rational mind, as your thoughts are always a result of your conscious and subconscious beliefs. Take a moment to observe if you feel lighter. Feeling lighter is usually a good sign that a negative bond has been resolved and cleared. When you feel that, know you have just freed up precious energy, energy which you can now employ for your goals.

Your Inner Voice – Friend or Foe

We all know what it feels like when our mean little inner voice, aka "monkey mind" takes over. Mine was particularly stubborn for months after I was swindled out of a business I had put my life savings into. Eventually I realized I had a choice: I could go on listening to my mean inner voice and be miserable, or I could turn my voice around to something positive, even if this required considerable courage and a lot of effort. It was a bit like when we choose between being physically inactive (and therefore more tired) or physically fit (and just a bit more tired, yet energized, after exercising). I chose to make the effort to observe my thoughts and turn them around.

Life is a choice. Our thoughts are our choice. Our power is found in our choices. So do you want to make a choice and transform that monkey brain into your best friend?

Exercise 6: Make Your Inner Voice Your Best Friend!

It takes a lot of practice and conditioning to turn negative chatter around. We need to create "muscle memory" to avoid limiting self-talk and to tame our monkey mind's power so it neither takes control of our lives, nor sabotages our success. One way to do this is to replace disempowering thoughts and questions with empowering "what if" questions.

You've probably heard of affirmations. Many coaches teach turning around our negative self-talk with positive affirmations, and this is a very powerful and useful tool. However, an empowering question is often more effective than a simple affirmation. In fact, your subconscious mind often reacts more benevolently to a question than to an affirmative statement.[7] Why? It rejects affirmations that are not supported by your belief system. So if you try to tell yourself an affirmation that your subconscious just doesn't believe, it really won't be beneficial, and it may even backfire. You need to be able to truly feel the affirmation. With a question, on the other hand, you open up a possibility and stimulate your mind to find solutions. Instead of focusing on the "problem," an empowering question turns your mind to look out for the positive aspects and opportunities in a situation, rather than the possible risks.

Let's do it! Write down 10 negative, disempowering thoughts you tend to have with regards to speaking in public, for example:

- *What if they don't like me?*
- *Maybe I will blank.*
- *What I have to say is not important enough.*
- *I'm too nervous!*
- *What if I fail?*
- *I may not be a good enough speaker.*
- *What if I mess up?*
- *I'm not articulate enough.*
- *What if I don't have the answers to all their questions?*
- *What if they think I'm a fraud because I'm not knowledgeable enough?*
- *What if everything goes wrong? Etc.*

Any of these sound familiar?

---

[7] Noah St. John, *The Secret Code of Success: 7 Hidden Steps to More Wealth and Happiness* (published by HarperCollins e-books), pg 53ff.

Once you have identified 10 disempowering thoughts or questions, flip them around into empowering "what if" questions:

- *What if they think I'm awesome?*
- *What if I do a great job?*
- *What if my talk will change someone's life?*
- *What if I could be calm?*
- *What if it feels amazing to share my unique gift?*
- *What if they are grateful for what I have to offer to them?*
- *What if I had more fans after my talk? Etc.*

Experiment with this and feel the difference between the two thought patterns. Ponder on how these change your outlook. Do you feel the magic in these questions? Are you looking forward to creating these results?

You can also use empowering questions to create a greater connection with your audience. For example:

- *How do I want my audience to feel?*
- *How can I best connect with my audience?*
- *How will their lives or careers improve through my product?*

These questions direct the focus away from you towards your audience, where your thoughts really should be because you don't go out there to speak to yourself. You speak to other people who need to hear your message. It's not about you. It's about them. Spending too much energy and thought on how nervous you are means you're putting all the attention on yourself. However, the issue is not how comfortable you are. It's about how comfortable the audience will be with you. So rather think about how you can connect with them, think about what you can do to make them feel at ease, to engage them and make this a memorable experience for them. Asking these empowering questions will help do so.

Once you've experienced the magical power of questions, go on to ask positive "why" questions. Allow them to catapult you directly into your creative self.

- *Why am I such a great speaker?*
- *Why am I doing such a great job with this audience?*
- *Why am I so successful?*

Even if you don't have all the answers to your "why" questions, your subconscious mind has something to work with now. Your subconscious is like an enormous filter. Every single second, there are so many impressions competing to make it into our mind that without this filter, we would go crazy. Depending on how it's programmed and stimulated, the subconscious prioritizes all the things going on around us and filters out what seems unimportant to it (even if it is what matters for your success.). Positive "why" questions motivate your filter to let in ideas and opportunities that favor the solutions to your questions. In his book, Noah St. John uses the term "Afformations" for these positively phrased why questions.[8]

When you're looking for additional inspiration to spice up your presentation, "what would it take" questions work well:

- *What would it take to engage my audience?*
- *What would it take for me to inspire my audience?*
- *What would it take to influence and impact my audience?*

Now you have a series of options to turn your disempowering thoughts around. No more excuses for having them swirl about in your mind! Always remember, what you focus on expands. What you put your attention to is what you get. This is because your subconscious mind works with what your conscious mind suggests to it. When you suggest a thought of blanking, it will "help" you create blanking. When you do it repeatedly, it creates a pattern. The good thing is that this also works the other way around. When you cultivate positive thoughts and questions, positive patterns are created in your life. Nice!

---

[8] Ibid.

PART II:
ONE WEEK BEFORE THE EVENT

Your event is one week away. Whether you're scheduled for a client presentation, a formal address or speech to a large audience, a workshop you're teaching, or a pitch to investors, it's essential to make the best out of the last few days before the event to psychologically brace yourself and avoid any last-minute crises or panic attacks.

Chapter 4

REHEARSING

From new ways of rehearsing to finding your magnetic power, the following exercises will equip you with a series of options to optimize your performance ahead of time. Integrate your preferred ones into your routine, so you can actually look forward to speaking up in meetings or in front of a room.

Visualization

Visualization is a powerful tool to manage your stage fright and to improve your performance, and makes it a wonderful rehearsal technique. Visualization has been used by the most successful Olympic athletes for decades.[9] Powerful mental images allowed Olympians to carry home their gold medals. According to a study conducted by Russian scientists with four groups of Olympic athletes, the group with the highest percentage of mental training (75%) showed the best performance.[10]

---

[9] Sarah Schmalbruch, "Here's The Trick Olympic Athletes Use to Achieve Their Goals," *Business Insider,* January, 28, 2015, http://www.businessinsider.com/olympic-athletes-and-power-of-visualization-2015-1.
[10] Ibid.

Imagination has been used by anyone who has ever invented something. Just think about the airplane; two brothers visualized human beings flying. At the time, people laughed at them; now we can't imagine a world without air travel. Visioning and visualizing is the first step to arriving where we want to be. Everything starts in our minds; everything starts with a vision. Thought precedes any material manifestation. You have to believe it to see it in the material world!

I often hear coaches say, "Dreams don't come true. Plans come true." Yes, but... there is no plan without a dream! There is no plan without a vision. Dreams or visions become plans, which then become action, and eventually results. You must have a vision first.

Why is visualization so powerful? Visualization puts your vision or dream out into the Universe, raises your vibration, and tells the Universe to start conspiring in your favor to bring in the right resources and connections at the right time and place. Your subconscious mind doesn't distinguish between physical reality and vivid imagination. Visualization fills the gap between what we already have and what we desire to have, between where we are and where we want to be. When we visualize what we want, we motivate our subconscious mind to watch out for the opportunities and people that help us move closer to our goal. These are often things we might not otherwise see. Additionally, visualization inspires our mind's creativity and stimulates idea generation and problem solving.

Visualization also modifies the filters of our subconscious mind. What we let into our mind is determined by our conscious and subconscious beliefs about ourselves and the world that surrounds us. When we visualize something positive, we change those filters to permit only positive beliefs. We start to observe more cases of positive synchronicity, like being at the right place at the right time. Last but not least, positive visualization raises our vibration so that we energetically attract the people and the resources necessary to achieve our goal and make our vision a physical reality.

Powerful visualizations require emotion. Your emotions and feelings play a major role in manifesting the results you desire. The more you feel into your mental movie, the more you lift your vibration. Your subconscious mind doesn't know the difference between what's really happening and what you envision. What you visualize seems just as real to your subconscious as what you perceive as your reality with your conscious mind. When you play a vision in your mind, your subconscious mind operates under cover, without you even realizing it, to come up with ideas that support your vision. It goes on a search for opportunities and actions that lead to its implementation. Through imagining your vision in your mind, you interrupt existing neural pathways and replace them with new, positive pathways, which generate new thought patterns. When you add powerful emotions and feelings to those visualizations, your subconscious creates firmer associations. This leads to the results you want to achieve.

Let's do a quick test of visualization. Make sure to only read the next paragraph before proceeding to the test.

Sit upright with your feet firmly planted on the floor. Now twist to your right side as far as you can. Observe how far you can twist; what does your right eye see? Remember that spot. Come back to center.

Done? Read on:

Close your eyes and imagine your head can go all the way around, 360 degrees, as if there was no natural block. See this movement in your mind for about 30 seconds. After those 30 seconds, open your eyes, and again twist to your right side as far as you can. What does your right eye see now?

Over 60% of all people I have guided through this experiment at live events report that their range of motion increases considerably the second time around, and most others confirmed that it had increased somewhat. This simple exercise demonstrates just how powerful visualization can be: Within a matter of a few seconds we can enhance our range of motion, just through visualizing. No physical effort or training required. It's the power of our minds.

I use visualization all the time. And I know you do, too! The question is, do you use it consciously or unconsciously. Do you imagine all the things you don't want to happen, like blanking or freezing in front of your audience or making a fool of yourself? Remember, we can't stop thinking but we can change our thoughts. We can't stop the movie in our heads but we can modify the image feed through visualization.

The article "Mental Rehearsal & Visualization: The Secret to Improving Your Game Without Touching a Basketball!" by Joe Haefner, describes Dr. Judd Biasiotto's study with basketball players at the University of Chicago.[11] First he divided the players into three groups and pre-tested them on their free-throw skills. Then he had one group practice an hour per day, he had another group visualize executing perfect free throws, and instructed the third group to do nothing at all. When he re-tested them after 30 days, the first group had improved by 24%, the second group by 23% (only training in their minds), and the third group didn't show any significant change. Both the physical training and the mental training generated almost the same outcome.[12] This is how powerful mental rehearsals are.

Similar results occurred with my own clients. When I started my coaching practice, I mostly worked with performing artists, mainly dancers, who found this practice priceless. In 2013, I was invited to speak at the International Dance Council's (Conseil International de la Danse - CID) World Congress in Athens, Greece, and on one of the last days, the participating dancers were rehearsing for a special performance at a nearby amphitheater. The floor was made of stone, and one of the two dancers of a duo was concerned about falling onto the hard, concrete-like floor while performing a specific move. I

---

[11] Joe Haefner, "Mental Rehearsal & Visualization: The Secret to Improving Your Game Without Touching a Basketball!" *Breakthrough Basketball*, accessed September 5, 2016,
https://www.breakthroughbasketball.com/mental/visualization.html.

[12] Ibid.

taught her how to rehearse the move mentally, visualizing herself successful and safe. Her performance turned out to be exceptionally smooth, and she walked away happy and unscathed. After the show, she ran over to me and said, "I rehearsed the movement over and over in my mind, and when the moment came, I just knew that I could do it." It's always amazing to hear these success stories.

Another client of mine was interviewing for a high-ranking marketing job. Before I taught her a specific visualization technique, she was disappointed because she had had several unsuccessful interviews despite her relevant background and previous TV appearances. As a result of practicing visualization, she got the job of her dreams. After the interview she told me, "Regina, I walked into that room and I knew the job was mine."

So, what does visualization have to do with preparing to speak up and stand out in any situation? The truth is that speakers are performers, and this tool can be equally valuable to you. I use visualization to create my mental rehearsal space and rehearse mentally. This helps me feel more confident and achieve better results easily, just like the Olympic and collegiate athletes. Let me guide you through a process that allows you to create your very own, personal rehearsal space.

Exercise 7: Create Your Mental Rehearsal Space
Find a comfortable sitting position. Close your eyes, take a few deep breaths, and relax. Deep relaxation intensifies your experience and favors mental re-programming. When we slow down our brain activity, we enter a theta state, which reduces our stress level (nice side effect), heightens our mental clarity, and increases our receptivity for learning. The following is an easy way to go into a theta state:

- Count from 1 to 10 and allow yourself to slowly move into deep relaxation:
- Soften and close your eyes, relax your jaw, relax all your face muscles
- Relax your neck and shoulders

- Relax your arms, hands, and fingers
- Relax your chest
- Relax your upper back, lower back, and sacrum
- Relax your stomach and belly
- Relax your legs, knees and feet
- Feel your feet connected to the floor, enjoy the feeling of being grounded
- Relax your entire body
- Feeling completely relaxed

Now that you are relaxed, let's visualize your mental rehearsal space. You will want to create your very specific, personal rehearsal space in your mind. This may be the room you're going to speak in, the stage you are going to speak on, your office, or any other space of your preference, such as a place in nature. It could even be an imaginary space, if that would serve you.

If you have a talk or presentation coming up and you have seen the venue, I highly recommend you visualize that space. This allows you to play your scene in the expected setting and your subconscious mind will register this as if you were already physically on that stage or in that space. This will help you get more familiar with the space over your rehearsal period, which will help you feel even more comfortable and confident when the time comes for you to talk from that stage.

Now imagine a door or a gate. This may be the door that leads to your actual venue, or it may be an imaginary door to your preferred place in nature or to your imaginary retreat. Take a moment to inspect the door/gate: What does it look like? What is it made of? Is it made of wood, of metal? Is it a two-winged door? A revolving door? A sliding door? If it's a gate, is it made of iron? Does it have a handle, a knob? The important thing isn't what the door looks like, but how well you visualize it. Go ahead and open it, then step over the threshold.

Take a look around. What does the space look like? Is it a stage? Is it a meeting room? What does the place smell like? What does it feel like? What do you hear? Maybe it even has a certain taste to it. Use all your senses! How big is it? Are there any props? What is the lighting like? Is there a microphone? Be sure you have a clear picture of this space in your mind! Make it as clear and colorful as if you were painting it on a canvas. If you have a hard time visualizing, listen to the sounds. Smell the air. Feel where you are.

Look at your audience. Who are they? Who is sitting in the front rows? What are their expectations, their hopes? What motivated them to show up? What do they want to learn from you? Allow them into your mental rehearsal space to make it more real; picture them as vividly as you can.

Once you have a solid image of your rehearsal space, you are ready to move into action with your mental rehearsal, where you will use this visualized rehearsal space over and over again.

Exercise 8: Mental Rehearsal to Raise Your Confidence

While visualizing your mental rehearsal space, walk in front of your audience or onto your stage. Look into your audience, pause, and take a deep breath. Don't skip this part, either in visualization or in real life! It not only helps you gather yourself, but also grabs your listeners' attention and draws them in before you even say a single word. This moment can be tremendously powerful. Use it! Include this initial deep breath in all your rehearsals so it becomes second nature. Only after that breath should you start speaking.

Imagine yourself speaking and moving gracefully and effortlessly. Visualize your best possible speaker self. Imagine the parts of your talk which were challenging before you got here are coming along quite naturally. Practice the entire talk as if you were playing a movie in your mind; take your time and enjoy speaking so effortlessly, freely and confidently. Picture yourself underlining your words with the appropriate body language, gestures, smiles, and eye contact. See yourself speaking just as you want yourself to be speaking during your speaking gig!

If you catch yourself making a mistake, just rewind and repeat that part. Replay it in your mind the way you'd like it to be. Make this experience as real as possible, being sure to visualize while keeping a positive state of mind. Observe what it feels like. Does it feel joyful? Do you feel passionate while you speak? Are you connecting with your audience? Are you integrating them into your talk?

Allow yourself to have a delightful experience as you rehearse. Remember, your state of mind creates your reality. The more pleasure you get from this visualization, the easier it will be to repeat an improved performance at your event. Your subconscious doesn't make a distinction of what you do in your mind and what you do physically, so picturing yourself speaking is a powerful and empowering tool. A mental rehearsal will increase your confidence both before you present and in the actual moment of speaking. It is essential to increased success when speaking up.

Now take the next two minutes to continue your talk or keep repeating the one part of it that you know you need to specifically focus on! See yourself successful.

Always add a good portion of enthusiasm and vigor to your mental rehearsals. A positive energy opens up your subconscious mind to opportunities coming your way. Our inner speech is a huge contributor to opening the subconscious, which then affects our results.

We often think, "When I have achieved this and that, I will be happy," but the Universe doesn't work that way. Most of us were brought up with the motto, "I'll believe it when I see it;" however, the Law of Attraction works the other way around: We see it when we believe it. We can only create what we believe we can create. Our beliefs create our reality, whether they are positive or negative. That's why it is imperative that when you visualize your rehearsals, you do so in a positive, high energy, high vibration state.

Vibrations match vibrations. Our vibration attracts a like vibration. So we have to feel happy first. Some people say, "Fake it till you make it." I like to say, "Feel it till you make it."

Feeling good is contagious. It's more fun to be around someone who emanates positive energy. And feeling good relieves stress and anxiety, both for yourself and your audience. Plus, it has a nice side effect: Feeling good raises your vibration for great things to happen.

Repeat your mental rehearsals at a high vibration often, especially the night before your gig!

Rehearse to Impress!

I don't have to remind you that practice and repeated rehearsals are key for a memorable talk. Very few people can wing it successfully. If you're one of them, congratulations! But if you were one of them, you probably wouldn't be reading this book.

The previous section showed you how to mentally rehearse for success. This section is about content rehearsal: how to remember your script, your flow, or possibly the actual words. Whether you use one or the other is a matter of preference and a matter of the duration of your speech or presentation. For instance, when I have been assigned a short speaker's slot of five minutes, I will make sure to rehearse word by word. On the other hand, when I'm preparing to teach a half-day workshop, word for word memorization would not make sense.

If you resist repetition because you're easily bored, then you're in good company. I, too, am easily bored. You'll have to come up with an incentive to trick yourself into rehearsing. The first thing you want to do is schedule rehearsal time. Put it on your calendar. Let's assume you have a 60- minute talk coming up in a month and you know you have to practice it at least 10 times. You may need more rehearsals, say 20 or 50, depending on how often you have delivered similar content, whether you're a native speaker, and how much practice you need to feel comfortable. Regardless of how often you need to rehearse, pencil rehearsal time into your calendar. Ideally you rehearse at the same time every single day to make it a routine, but if that's not possible, I recommend you find a time during the day when you typically focus pretty well. For me, late mornings or early afternoons are best, once I've dealt with urgent stuff and email. For you it may be different. Once you have practice time scheduled, you need to inspire yourself to follow through.

As a little girl, I dreaded Sundays in the winter because I was always bored. There was not a lot to do in the German village I grew up in, except for playing with the snow, and we only did that if there was any snow and the weather was nice enough. We did not have as many leisure options for cold, dreary weather as we have nowadays: there were no nearby museums, and it was never in our plan to go to the movies. As a result of my winter boredom, there was a time in my life when I filled every single minute of my day, just so I wouldn't have a chance to be bored. I easily get weary of repetitive routines, and it requires a good amount of discipline for me to stick with them.

So, I get it. As someone who dreads boredom, I'm not a huge fan of repetition, and I have a tough-love relationship with rehearsals. But I know repetition is the mother of skill, so I do it anyway.

If you are like me and frequently don't feel like practicing, here's a way to turn your rehearsal aversion around by replacing your apathetic thoughts with inspiring questions.[13]

Exercise 9: Inspire Yourself to Practice

Some examples of apathetic thoughts are "I really don't feel like rehearsing today!" and "Rehearsing is boring!"

Start by dividing a piece of paper into two columns and jot down your own apathetic thoughts in the left column.

Once that's finished, turn the apathetic thoughts around into inspiring questions, writing your new questions in the right column, for instance:

- *Why is it so much fun pretending that my audience is already in front of me and I'm speaking to them?*
- *Why do I love speaking/teaching so much?*
- *Why do I enjoy acting out my talk?*
- *Why is it getting easier and easier for me to speak in front of an audience?*
- *Why am I feeling so inspired to speak today?*

Remember, when we ask an inspiring or empowering question, our subconscious mind starts working on a solution. It will support us in our endeavors to find the answer to that question. Let's say we

---

[13] Noah St. John, *The Secret Code of Success: 7 Hidden Steps to More Wealth and Happiness.*

ask "Why do I enjoy rehearsing?" In this case, our subconscious mind will look for a reason why rehearsing could actually be enjoyable, and this motivates us to do it.

Now all you have to do is make sure the rehearsals actually happen. Here's what I like to do: Weather permitting, I take long walks in the park, plug my earphones in, and off I go talking to myself. My headset saves me from being locked up as a crazy lady chatting with herself. They also allow me to record changes right into my audio memos app. Script in my hands, I walk and walk and walk, and I talk and talk and talk, until eventually I don't need my script anymore. Speaking out loud is much different from repeating the words in silence. It allows you to discover what doesn't flow or sound good and to practice certain vocal qualities and intonations, so be sure to speak aloud. Focus on articulating clearly. A walk in the park keeps me from getting distracted and washing the dishes instead of rehearsing. Cleaning the house, otherwise much dreaded, comes in as a handy excuse to avoid practicing!

Rehearsing is also important to test and adapt the timing of your talk. While you may have an idea of the timing as you look at the length of your script, interactive parts, like when you ask questions, and other special effect sections may take longer than you think. We often underestimate the length of these parts in our timing when we don't play them out in our mind. Of course, even the best planners will have to manage interactive time during the actual talk as well as make sure to stay within schedule, but having a clear idea of how much time is reasonable for each part helps.

For best results, combine the two rehearsals. Use your imagination also while practicing your script: Don't only rehearse for yourself. In your mind, include the audience in your rehearsal and imagine a positive outcome. It makes it much more fun, and rehearsing mentally and emotionally with all the elements of a real experience makes your spoken rehearsal more effective.

Chapter 5

IMPROVING CONFIDENCE AND PERSONAL POWER

Even if you are rehearsing and consciously know you are well-prepared, subconscious fears may still sneak in and make you worry about the event itself. We talked about fears earlier and how they are not always rational nor useful. Fears make us worry. They project us out into a future we can't control instead of allowing us to stay present in the moment. When we worry, we imagine a negative outcome in the future that hasn't even happened. That's why we need some ways to deal with fear and worries quickly and effectively.

Getting Rid of Worries

I used to be such a worrier, but worrying never led me anywhere good. It only took up precious energy that I could have employed to create greater results. We should be really careful what we worry about, because it might come true... Remember, we're such great manifestors. We constantly create our own reality through our beliefs and our thoughts and our emotional patterns. The question is this: are we manifesting what we want, or are we manifesting things we don't really want because we worry and fear too much. What we focus on expands. If you focus on positive thoughts, you will create more positive results. If you worry too much, those negative thoughts will most likely come to fruition in the real world.

Exercise 10: Count out Your Worries

When you find yourself worrying, I suggest you do this exercise. Before you start, set an intention to switch to a positive state of mind and create an image of what this should look like. For example, you could intend to come up with three easy-to-accomplish action steps you can take to create a positive outcome. Write them down, indulge in the fun, then move to action.

All you need to do is count down to 0 from 200 by subtracting 7:

$$200 - 7 = 193 - 7 = 186, \text{ etc.}$$

It seems simple, but it's effective. I did not invent this technique; therapists have been using it for many years. Concentrating on a math task helps us neutralize our thoughts because it's impossible to think negative thoughts and do math at the same time.

I found the same is true when I take dance classes that require all my focusing abilities to integrate the movements and choreographic sequence at the same time. If you are like me, you will prefer dance to math. You can try the following exercise instead of mathematics to rid yourself of worries.

Exercise 11: Dance Away the Blues

Whenever I find myself worrying, my best therapy is practicing some complex dance moves. Whether it's a live dance class or a YouTube video, a dance break always makes me feel better. When I add complexity to my dancing, I am forced to concentrate on the task at hand and I automatically stop worrying.

Now that you have set the foundation of a strong speaking performance by moving into a positive state of mind, let's shift gears and get you to the next step on your way towards excellence! Would you like to feel more confident before you get on stage? I'm about to show you how to strengthen your self-belief, fervor, and magnetism, so you can leave your worrier self behind and step into your warrior speaking self instead.

Confidence at Your Fingertips

When one of my dream projects busted some years ago, my confidence fell below zero. At the time I let myself be devastated by circumstances. Re-building my confidence from a level that low required time and arduous focus. I needed a tool that would allow me to slip into a confident version of myself instantly when the stakes were high. Between Neuro-Linguistic Programming (NLP) classes and holistic wellness sessions, I learned how to anchor a feeling of happiness. Both experiences led me to develop the following exercise:

Exercise 12: Trigger a Feeling of Confidence

This exercise allows you to easily and quickly shift your state of mind from fear to confidence, from freaking out to freaking amazing!

I will show you how to anchor a feeling of confidence, so you can trigger confidence whenever you need to.

The trigger is a specific hand gesture of your choosing. This gesture should be something that you don't usually do, as it should only be used for this purpose. It must be easy to do, and you should be able to do it discreetly so you can use it under any circumstances without feeling awkward. It could be snapping your fingers or making a fist. Please take a moment to choose a gesture now so you have it ready when it's time to use it.

We will be creating an association between your chosen gesture and the feeling of confidence. This will allow you to switch into a confident state of mind whenever you need to, simply by doing the gesture.

First, move into deep relaxation:

- Soften and close your eyes, relax your jaw, relax all your face muscles

- Relax your neck and shoulders
- Relax your arms, hands, and fingers
- Relax your chest
- Relax your upper back, lower back, and sacrum
- Relax your stomach and belly
- Relax your legs, knees and feet
- Feel your feet connected to the floor, enjoy the feeling of being grounded
- Relax your entire body
- Feeling completely relaxed

Now follow along with me:

Think of a time in your life when you enjoyed a high level of self-esteem or during which you experienced the most confidence ever. Allow yourself to travel in time and to glide back into that situation. Now re-live that scene. What did it feel like, look like, smell like, sound like? Really take a few minutes to cherish and savor that moment when you felt so wonderfully confident and courageous. What made you feel that way? What sensations went through your body when you felt that way? Where in your body did you feel that confidence? Cherish all the delightful sensations and emotions that are coming up! Give yourself permission to get intense with it! How intensely can you feel this confidence? Linger there until you get the strongest sensation of confidence you possibly can.

When it is getting most intense, use your hand gesture to anchor that feeling. This causes your body to create an association between the anchor and the feeling. You just conditioned your physiology to create the feeling of confidence every time you use your hand gesture.

Take a couple of deep breaths, then open your eyes.

You may need to repeat the entire exercise several times with the trigger so your body gets conditioned to it and remembers it. Test it until it becomes easy to connect to the feeling of confidence automatically every time you use your hand gesture.

If you use your anchor regularly, it will maintain its strength. If not, you will need to repeat this exercise from time to time to bring it back into your cell memory. In the future, you'll be able to re-create that same feeling of confidence whenever you need it, just by using this hand gesture. You won't have to go through the entire visualization each time, just use the hand gesture. In a matter of seconds, you will be able to move into a confident state of mind. Isn't that amazing?

An Executive Assistant, who attended a session where I taught this technique, called me a couple of weeks later and said: "I was skeptical, but I decided to practice an open mind and test it. I have to say, it really works! I now use this exercise every time a challenge comes up in my job and even in my personal life."

By the way, you may want to use this exercise to conjure up any other desired feelings and states of mind, such as happiness, courage, joy. Just make sure you use a different hand gesture for each different emotion.

Find Your Magnetic Power
Magnetic power is about charisma and that unique appeal we discussed earlier; it is that magic spell some people seem to naturally exude. Do you think of yourself as magnetic? Who comes to mind when you think of magnetic power? What makes them magnetic to you? Why do you feel drawn to them?

Magnetic power is closely related to your self-image and your attitude. We are usually drawn to people who are enthusiastic, who engage us and make us feel special; these are people who listen and are present while speaking with us, and who emanate certainty about what they say while being warm and relatable.

In order to become magnetic to others, it helps to feel your own magnetic power first.

For the longest time, I felt like others got more attention than me. I didn't feel magnetic at all. I felt I was not important enough, not pretty enough, not interesting enough to deserve attention. As a teenager, I was certainly not aware of my power. I lived in the future, in my dreams for the life I would create for myself. My dreams were a way to escape the present moment. Looking back, I feel this is why I wasn't magnetic. When we're not in the present moment, it's impossible to be magnetic. As soon as I chose to live in the present I was able to increase my magnetic power and bring to myself what I desired.

Are you looking to make your talks, presentations, or pitches more engaging? Would you like to draw a larger audience towards you or get more attention for your suggestions during meetings? Would you like to enhance your magnetism by doing what I did? Let's get started.

Exercise 13: Acknowledge Your Power
For this exercise, you will need a piece of paper, a pen, and a mirror.

Take a sheet of paper and write the following sentence starters at the top, one on the left and one on the right:

"I am uniquely powerful and I know this because... [fill in the blank]."

"I have magnetic power and I know this because... [fill in the blank]."

Under each, write down the supporting statements that come to mind to finish these sentences.

Read through all of the statements and choose the one that speaks to you the most. Now take the mirror, look yourself in the eyes, and say that statement out loud until you begin to believe it deep down in your heart.

Observe what happens. If this makes you emotional, I suggest you work with an expert so you can clear your subconscious fears and limiting beliefs around your own unique power. It is an investment that always pays off.

Even if it doesn't make you emotional, repeat the exercise several times and observe what thoughts and feelings come up. Do these statements trigger any doubts or do you have a hard time filling in the blank? If so, there's always the option of starting with a "why" question first: "Why am I so uniquely powerful?" or "Why do I have so much magnetic power?" Observe what comes up for you and then go back to the original exercise as described above.

Another way of coming up with great options for the blank in statement "I am uniquely powerful and I know this because..." is to make a list of 50 accomplishments. We often don't acknowledge ourselves enough. We admire others for what they achieve, but we don't see our own achievements as achievements. Writing down a list of our feats and triumphs allows us to see our own value. Taking stock of what we have already accomplished in our lives increases our trust in what we can achieve in the future, starting now.

You are getting closer to your event. Take a moment to revise what you have learned about optimally preparing for your event. Check in with yourself. Have you persuaded yourself that your message is worth transforming your fear into courage? Have you connected with your limitless power? Have you tested and chosen your favorite tools to vamp up your confidence? Assess your progress and acknowledge yourself for it. How are you feeling? Be honest with yourself. Did you only read through the exercises or did you actually use them? How often? Do you need to rehearse more? If so, don't put it off; do it now.

PART III:
THE DAY AND NIGHT BEFORE THE EVENT

You now have a number of tools under your belt that allow you to turn speaking anxiety into excitement, resistance into fervor, and worries into positive expectation. Now it's all about making sure you make the most out of your last preparation day and get a good night's rest.

Chapter 6

PRACTICAL PREPARATIONS

Sometimes we become so absorbed in our content we forget to attend to the many details that go into our outfit. Has it ever been a couple of hours before your event and you can't find intact panty hose or your perfect green tie or you discover your shirt has a red wine stain? Or perhaps your iron broke and the cleaner's shop is closed? This has happened to me! Gladly a lovely neighbor helped me out with her iron. The lesson I learned was to check my complete outfit ahead of time. Avoid unnecessary last-minute stress.

Spice up Your Presence, and Your Confidence Will Follow

When you prepare for your presentation, remember to dress for success! What does that mean? Well, it means something different for every single person. If you are an entrepreneur, your outfit needs to be in alignment with your brand. You also want to dress to distinguish yourself. You want to dress to express your truth and to impress your audience. I like to tell people, "Express to impress!" Make an instant impact and leave a lasting impression by wearing your brand in a powerful, expressive way that makes you memorable.

This doesn't mean you have to go crazy, but if your brand is bad-ass, your outfit has to be bad-ass. If you are a fitness coach, you may want to wear cool gym clothes that accentuate your athletic body. If you are a fashion stylist who specializes in elegant outfits, show up that way! If you are a hair stylist or a make-up artist, make sure we see that in your own hair cut or make-up. As a corporate executive, your outfit may look different, depending on your industry. People in tech tend to dress less formally than bankers or lawyers, but gladly we are in a time where it's ok to wear a statement piece in about any environment, like a green tie, a red dress or an attention-grabbing bracelet. (Speaking of jewelry, you want to make sure your accessories don't divert people's attention away from your content, so don't wear jewelry that makes noise when you speak.)

In some instances, being aligned with the event may overrule being aligned with your brand. For instance, when you speak to a corporate audience in their own environment, you may need to consider their specific dress code. When in doubt about what to wear, check with them before the event. Studies show that people dressing up formally increases their thinking and focusing abilities.[14] Clothes change the wearers' self-perception. The same is true of dressing powerfully for your speaking gig.

Make sure you look and feel comfortable in your clothes. I find it highly disconcerting when women wear tight, pointy shoes that look like they are killing them; I feel like I can't focus on what they're saying when I see them teeter around as if they were walking on raw eggs. I love high heels for speaking, as they can make us feel more powerful, but my shoes absolutely have to be comfortable. When I teach an all-day workshop, I bring a second pair of heels to switch into half way through the day; changing shoes always feels good when standing for such a long time.

---

[14] Sandra Blakeslee, "Mind Games: Sometimes a White Coat Isn't Just a White Coat," *The New York Times Company*, April 2, 2012, http://www.nytimes.com/2012/04/03/science/clothes-and-self-perception.html?_r=0.

Prepare Your Outfit and Everything You Need to Take to the Venue

The day before your gig, make sure you set aside some time to prepare your outfit: clothes, shoes, accessories. Check that everything is clean and in good condition. Double check that the outfit fits well and that your shoes are comfortable enough to stand as long as you need. You don't want to have to worry about any of this while you are speaking, presenting, pitching or applying for a job.

Print your handouts, script, and any promotional materials you plan to take. In one corner of your office or living room, make a pile of all the items you will need at your meeting or gig before going to bed. If your event is a speaking engagement, I have a *Speaker's Checklist* available for instant download on my website at www.transformyourperformance.com/speakerchecklist.

Chapter 7

PRESENCE IN MIND, BODY AND ENERGY

As you prepare to speak, it is important to be present in your mind, your body and your energy. Being present in the moment is crucial to pushing away fear and anxiety. When we feel fear, we're actually projecting out to the future. When we step in front of a room or on a stage we want to be present in the moment, not living somewhere in the future. A quick and easy way to become more grounded and bring ourselves back to the present when our nerves run a little wild is deep breathing and simply focusing on your breath. Deep breathing alleviates any anxiety and tension you may feel in your body, and it calms your nerves. Focusing on your breath transmits a feeling of safety to your body and mind. Here's an easy way to breathe away those fears:

Exercise 14: Breathe Your Anxiety into Excitement

Close your eyes. Inhale deeply and bring the air all the way down to your belly. It's key to breathe deeply enough for your belly to stick out as you inhale and fill it with air. Hold your breath for a few seconds as you sip in some more air. While exhaling, imagine your belly button touching your spine. Repeat for five to ten breaths. Then observe how you feel. If your breath is usually shallow, this could even make you a bit dizzy. No worries, this is momentary; it's just your body reacting to the unusual (but healthier) breathing. Deep respiration releases toxins in your body and raises your energy level, as more oxygen reaches your cells and "wakes them up." It makes you feel more alive and relieves stress caused by fear.

Whenever you feel fear, don't suppress it, even when you don't have a whole lot of time to work your way through it. Instead, breathe into your fear. Feel its intensity; feel the power in your fear feeling. Breathe into your fear and your anxiety until it turns into excitement. Yes, you can turn your fear around with your breath. Don't believe it? Try it! It works.

Set an Intention

Now it's time to set an intention for your speaking engagement. What do you want to get out of your gig? Set a clear intention for your event. Your intention could be to inspire the audience to take action to change a certain aspect of their lives, to motivate 50 people to sign up for your mailing list or for your coaching program, to sell your company's new tech product to a retailer, to raise capital for your project, etc. Whatever it is, be clear and specific about it! And write it down! When we write an intention or a goal down, it becomes easier to achieve it.

Meditate with Positive Mantras

Meditating with positive mantras is another awesome way to get rid of any negativity you may feel the night before your big speaking engagement. Many people write down their own mantras, record them, then listen to them to bring in positivity. As you repeat the mantras, your subconscious mind gets rewired with positive message bits, which ultimately form new and more empowering belief systems. As you bring new thoughts to your mind and reinforce them through repetition, outdated neural connections and networks are disconnected and replaced with new, more enabling connections and networks. Isn't that awesome? It's really reassuring to know that we are not hard-wired!

By the way, you can also search for a ready-made guided meditation. Guided meditations are an excellent alternative if you find it challenging to quiet your mind with traditional meditation, which in moments of performance anxiety can be more frustrating than calming. There are several apps with free guided meditations like Calm and Omvana, and YouTube is also a great source.

The following are some mantras I like to use:

- *I am powerful.*
- *I am hot stuff.*
- *I am enough.*
- *I love myself.*
- *The more I love myself, the more love I have to give.*
- *I am an open channel for creativity.*
- *Creative ideas flow through me.*
- *Every day I am getting better and better in so many ways.*
- *Everything I need is within me.*
- *I am now connected with my inner power.*
- *I expand in abundant wealth and inspire others to do the same.*
- *It's perfectly ok for me to have everything I want.*
- *It's safe to stand in the spotlight and to get attention.*
- *I am open to receiving what I most desire.*
- *My services are valuable and benefit others.*
- *With my business, I change people's lives.*
- *I follow the divine plan of my life.*
- *I am exactly where I am supposed to be, moving steadily forward.*
- *I am grateful for the opportunities each day offers to me.*
- *It is my birthright to use my unique talents and gifts every single day.*
- *It is my responsibility and my wish to share my wisdom and to shine my light out to the world.*
- *I am creating miracles for myself while I am helping others at the same time.*
- *I am richly rewarded for the work I do and the message I share.*
- *I am in the attitude of gratitude.*
- *My life is blossoming.*
- *I am ready for success.*

Remember to use meditation to rid the negativity from yourself when you need it. Find the mantras or statements that sound and feel the most appealing to you and direct all your energy to them. Awaken the dormant greatness inside yourself so others can see it in you as well. Ultimately, how you come across is a reflection of how you feel deep inside about yourself and what you bring to the table to make a difference for the people whose lives you get to touch through your presentation, your contribution in a meeting, your motivational speech, as a teacher or as a speaking activist.

It's time to get some rest so you can wake up refreshed. The following exercise allows you to fall asleep on a positive note.

Allow Yourself to Dream

When I was little, I was such a dreamer. Dreams were my preferred world. In my dreams, I could create whatever I wanted. My favorite place for imagination time was the bathtub! I'd lock myself in the bathroom, sit in the empty bathtub and pretend that this was my world where I could have anything I desired. Admittedly, my dreams at the time were quite modest like traveling to the ocean or having my own room. Only later did I dream about living in my own elegant mansion in Italy. Now my dreams are completely different. Clearly, dreams change over a lifetime, but they are powerful in every stage.

Unfortunately, most of us were educated out of dreaming. "Dreamer" was not a positive label when I was a young girl, and it isn't often associated with a positive connotation today. We are supposed to face reality to get prepared for "the world out there" and a life of hard work. So many of us unlearned the art of dreaming and visioning because of similar imposed beliefs. We suppressed our attention to our inner world in favor of the outer world, forgetting that the latter is a result of the former. Now we know that there's no plan without a vision; no reality without a dream. So let's go back to be that dreamer and dream ourselves to success.

You deserve to stand in the limelight. You are entitled to your big dream of being a famous motivational speaker, an activist that changes the world, a corporate leader who brings in more business with your presentation, or whatever your dream role is. What could this role ideally look like at tomorrow's gig? Dreaming of a successful interaction with your intended audience is one of the best ways you can prepare the night before your event.

Exercise 15: Dream Yourself to Success

Close your eyes. Picture the venue of your event in your mind. Now imagine your audience. They are joining you tomorrow because they are eager to hear what you have to share. They need to hear your message; they are hungry for what you have to offer. And you know you have important wisdom to share which will benefit them. They want you to succeed because they want to get the most for their time and money. This doesn't mean they want you to be perfect. They just want to get the value you can provide to them. And you can, because you are the expert in your field and you have a myriad of valuable insights to share with them. They are attending this event because they know they will walk away with value and learn something from you. And you know they will.

Step outside yourself. This is not about you. They are the ones who will benefit from your presentation and the reason why you are on stage. Take a moment to internalize this. During your talk, you let them feel that they are the reason you are there by asking questions and allowing them to participate. You make the presentation all about them, which reduces your speaking anxiety.

Take a moment to acknowledge this appreciative audience. They are hanging on each of your words as you present your content, as you share your story. It is okay to be vulnerable. As you allow yourself to be vulnerable, they connect with you deeply. You ask questions, and they are eager to participate because this topic is truly relevant to their lives and careers. See in your mind's eye how easy it is to engage and connect with them.

Some people nod in agreement during your talk; they all pay close attention to your words and your presentation. They appreciate you for doing this, for sharing your wisdom, for having the courage to be on that stage or in front of that room.

It's the end of your talk and people applaud with appreciation. You revel in that applause for a while and enjoy the feeling of a successful presentation.

Tailor this visualization as needed, adding specifics from your speaking engagement to the visualization. For the rest of the night, continue dreaming about this enjoyable event, and wake up refreshed and enthusiastic about a new day filled with opportunities.

PART IV:
THE DAY OF THE EVENT

Your big day is here. This part gives you some tips of how to best spend the hours leading up to your event. If this is your first client presentation, your first time speaking in front of a large audience, or your first pitch, this day can be a bit stressful. Whether you are an entrepreneur or have a job, make sure you clear your schedule, which allows you to relax and mentally prepare for your gig. From the following options, choose the ones that are within your possibilities and preferences. Above all, create a stress-free and pleasant day for yourself and cultivate a positive outlook for your gig.

Chapter 8

Practice Tranquility and Mental Alertness

Acompelling attitude and a positive energy are essential to a successful speaking experience. Choosing activities that ease your tension, enhance your self-trust and increase your mental focus will bring you feelings of serenity and tranquility. Doing so will brighten the experience for you and your audience.

Self-care

When you step into the spotlight, you want to be and show the best version of yourself. That requires taking optimum care of yourself. The day of the talk is not the best moment to rehearse everything over and over again. This should happen in the last few days and weeks. Instead, use the hours preceding your presentation to indulge in self-care, while always leaving enough time to get dressed, have your hair and make-up or any other necessary preparations done, and arrive early.

Self-care looks different for everyone and depends on your speaking or meeting schedule and how much time you have available that day. Maybe a massage is the best way for you to relax and feel calm and serene. Maybe you prefer a work-out or a walk in the park. Maybe you meditate. There's no right or wrong, as long as the activity serves your goal of calming your nerves and feeling zen and energized at the same time. And definitely add your favorite tools from this book.

Feel Delightful

Your state of mind changes how you show up for your meeting or presentation. People sense it when you feel good about being there, and it's just more fun to be around a speaker or meeting partner who obviously is enjoying the experience. This pleasant exercise helps you shift your state of mind from worried to cheerful in those moments leading up to your event.

Exercise 16: Indulge in a Delightful Memory

Close your eyes and focus on a delightful experience for 30 seconds. This may be eating your favorite ice cream, hugging someone you love, diving in a beautiful underwater scenery, enjoying a fresh breeze on a sailboat, or something else entirely. The image that works best for me is to hold a vision of me dancing with my favorite dance partner. It instantly takes me to a state of bliss. Don't forget to smile while you do this! Now, open your eyes and notice how you feel.

Before you go on, make a list of three delightful, joyful experiences you can use for this exercise, so they're ready when you need them.

Feel free to use this exercise whenever you want to feel more joyful, not only before you go on stage or into a meeting.

Power Posing

Most people have heard of Amy Cuddy. She is an Associate Professor at Harvard Business School, but most people know her for her TED talk on power posing.[15] (If you haven't seen it, definitely check it out on YouTube!) Through extensive research, Cuddy discovered that holding yourself in a confident way makes you feel more confident. It changes the way you show up for almost everything: networking, a meeting, a date, a sales conversation, a speaking gig. Cuddy explains that holding an expansive, big power

---

[15] Cuddy, A. (2012, June 28). Amy Cuddy: Your body language shapes who you are [Video file]. Retrieved from
https://www.ted.com/talks/amy_cuddy_your_body_language_shapes_who_you_are#t-88479.

pose for a couple of minutes raises your confidence level significantly.

Just as negative thoughts and feelings eventually show up as disease in our bodies (such as discomfort, pain, sickness, rashes, and deformations), a small posture decreases our confidence. However, a simple change in posture changes our feelings, thoughts, and confidence. It goes in both directions; it's a two-way cause and effect chain.

Let's experiment. Smile and hold it for 10 seconds. What happens? Do you feel a bit happier? Most people do, because smiling sends a signal to your brain that says: "happy," and your brain responds by sending those feelings throughout your body.

Exercise 17: Strike a Power Pose

This same principle applies to power posing: Holding a powerful pose tells your brain you are confident and in charge. In turn, your brain signals your body to feel confident and helps you stand confidently in your power.

If you never experimented with power posing, try it right now! Start with a disempowering posture like slouching and observe what that feels like: Do you feel small, contracted, unimportant? Now choose a power pose, e.g. the winning athlete's pose, the wonder woman pose, or the superman pose. Slowly move from your slouch into your preferred power pose and hold it for two minutes. Observe how you feel now. Do you feel more powerful?

When you "act as if" you feel more powerful and more confident, you start to really feel those states. Remember our subconscious doesn't distinguish between reality and something vividly imagined. Power posing will help you "fake it till you feel it," and before you know it, reality will catch up!

Power Dancing

While I am a fan of Amy Cuddy's Power Posing, I came up with Power Dancing as an alternative for myself, simply because I love dance.

Exercise 18: Dance into Your Power

Here's what Power Dancing looks like when I do it: I put on a power song, and I dance to it with big, powerful movements. Sometimes, I sing. Both dancing and singing release oxytocin, a neuropeptide that is produced in the hypothalamus and alleviates stress and anxiety, reduces social fear, and increases trust.[16] So when I power dance and sing, I increase my power and decrease my anxiety. Power Dancing makes me feel as if I literally embody my confidence. So many wins for me!

I have found that adding the joy factor of music is even more energizing and uplifting to me than power posing. It has become a great way to tap into my power. This may be true for you, or something entirely different could be the perfect fit for you finding your power and relieving stress. I bet you have your own ways to feel powerful. What makes you feel powerful? You probably have your own power tools. What are they? Whatever works to reduce stress and short-circuit nervousness is what you want to embrace and incorporate into your pre-speaking routine. Feel free to write them down and use them as needed.

Connect with Your Power

When I speak about power, I mean inner power. All we need to be successful is already inside of us. It took me a long time to learn that, and I had to go through some extremely painful experiences as a result. When I was swindled out of a business because of a dishonest business partner, I felt as if I'd handed my power over to my partner. In truth, I was just disconnected from my power. Our power stays with us at all times; we're just not always connected with it, or we simply forget about our power. We focus on external, possibly

---

[16] Sara McDonald, "Dancing to Boost Oxytocin," *The Mother Magazine*, last modified September 16, 2015, http://www.themothermagazine.co.uk/dancing-boost-oxytocin/.

unfavorable circumstances and live in a scary future instead of being present in the moment and in our power. We compare ourselves to others, wasting precious energy that we could use to become a superior version of ourselves. It is when we forget about, or become disconnected from, our power that we feel victimized, fearful, and insecure.

Once I fully understood this concept about personal power, I started strengthening my focus and faith in my inner power. That's when things started shifting for me. It began slowly at first, then started to snowball. Progress was made on the sale of the business property, which had been stuck for a while. I started preparing to move, and I began thinking about building a new future instead of just cleaning up the mess my business partner left behind. Translation jobs showed up to bridge the income situation, at least partially. Over time, the recovery process accelerated as I connected more intentionally to my inner power. Now I'm at a time where opportunities arise every single day and I am so grateful. When opportunities and successes don't show up for me, I know my focus is off and I need to re-adjust my connection to my personal power to keep moving in the right direction!

It hasn't been an easy process for me. My brain is a crazy chatterbox, generating a lot of noise and constantly working to distract me from my goals. It has taken a lot of practice, and I'm not a master yet. I've had to put in a lot of work to re-train my brain and reclaim my inner power through a more vibrant mindset. Fortunately, all the hard work and diligence has paid off in successes and deeper fulfillment.

It's key to remind ourselves daily that we all have all this power inside of ourselves: creative power, feminine/masculine power, personal power, heart power, the power of voice, the power of expression, the power of intuition and inner wisdom. And the best part is, this power is unlimited!

All we have to do is tap into this immense power and infinite potential, which is already inside of us, and we'll begin manifesting results in the material world. We have to connect with our power and embrace it in order to activate it. It's like an inner fire that is just waiting to be sparked. Without activating it, it's like using an unplugged TV set. We've got to plug the cord into the power outlet so power and energy can flow. When we activate our inner power, it can manifest in our outer world. So how do we activate our inner power? Let me show you.

Exercise 19: Tap into Your Inner Power

...and shine your brilliance out to the world!

If you prefer, you can watch my YouTube video *Connect with Your Inner Power (Strategic Minds Show)* and play along with me, or simply follow the below instructions:

Stand comfortably with your knees slightly bent and relax your shoulders. Close your eyes and take a few deep breaths to center and ground yourself. Feel your feet grounded on the floor and rooted into the Earth. Now feel the energy of the Earth flowing through the soles of your feet, up through your legs and into your torso. Let the Earth energy nurture you while you continue to take deep breaths.

Feel the Earth's energy coming up to the base of your spine; this is your support center. Take a moment here to feel supported and observe if this allows you to feel more grounded. Then bring the energy up to your belly area; this is where your creative power is located. Inhale deeply into your belly, and as you exhale, imagine your belly button touching your spine. Repeat for two more breaths.

Now bring the energy up into your stomach area, your solar plexus area. This is your personal power center. Place one or both hands on your solar plexus area and breathe into that area. Take a moment to feel and focus on your very own personal power! What you focus on, expands. Allow your mind to focus on your inner power and help it spread out from your solar plexus, and trust that it will!

Let the energy continue to flow from your solar plexus area up to your heart. Keep breathing and take a moment to open up your heart;

observe what that feels like. An energetically open heart helps you connect more deeply with your audience. An open heart allows others to trust you more.

Then let this energy flow through your throat; feel that area open up. This power center, the throat area, is related to self-expression and speaking our truth. A properly activated throat center allows you to speak your truth, express your ideas, and share your wisdom.

Now feel the energy coming up through your mouth into your head, flowing through your head and skull and into the energy field that surrounds your body. The field around your body is now filled up with this vibrant energy; it's as if you are surrounded by a bubble of powerful, radiating energy.

Pause. Take a moment to observe what this feels like and focus back on your solar plexus area. Feel the personal power there expand out into your energy bubble.

When you are finished, reflect on how you felt physically, emotionally and energetically during this exercise. Did your posture change at all? Did you become taller? Did you open your chest area? Did you feel more powerful, more confident, more energized and vibrant?

The goal of this exercise is for you to experience your enormous intrinsic value and to connect to your unlimited inner power. Feeling powerful from the inside raises your self-esteem. It also enhances your physical and energetic presence and how others perceive you. These are all things you want when you get in front of any type of audience.

Some of my clients used this technique before a job interview and they reported amazing results:

- "I didn't have my tongue tied as usual when talking to seniors."

- "During the previous interviews, nerves had been what messed it up. This time, I was calm and centered."
- "I said things that surprised me. I sounded so powerful all of a sudden."
- "The moment I walked into this room, I knew I'd get this job."

My clients aren't the only ones who have used this with such success. I personally use this inner power technique every single time I step in front of an audience or into an important meeting, and it has been a catalyst for my success as a speaker.

Saying "Yes" to Your YES Power

At networking events, I often hear, "You are always so positive," and "It's always great to have your smile in the room." In fact, someone recently said, "I thought there was something special about you because you smiled at every single person when they got up to introduce themselves." I've found it's more fun to be around people who smile more, so I try to smile frequently. Even if everyone doesn't appreciate my smile, it's definitely more fun to be around myself when I smile more.

I am German, and we can be brutally blunt and serious. One good thing about this is that our smiles are genuine. It just doesn't come easy to us to put on a fake smile. And it wouldn't work anyway. People feel when you're being fake. A sincere smile comes from within, and is felt energetically by those who receive it. Natural smiles come from our positive YES energy, which is a result of your conscious and subconscious consent to feeling cheerful and radiant. The conscious decision to upgrade your vibration is easy. The challenge comes with the subconscious part, and that's where the exercises of this book come in, so being in high spirits becomes more of a natural state over time.

Now, our days don't always go as we want them to go. There are circumstances that are out of our control and unpleasant things happen. Traffic jams, grumpy people on the subway, someone bumping into you in the street, maybe even learning some shocking and painful news are all possibilities on any given day. The day of your speaking event is not any different: Anything can happen. When you feel stressed by what's going on around you, take a moment to pause and come back to the present moment. Take a deep breath and ask yourself, "Does being stressed really serve me? Does it solve the situation?" I bet the answer is, "No." Make a decision to move into your positive YES energy to feel happy and radiant instead.

Here's a quick and effective exercise to do this:

Exercise 20: Move into Your Positive YES Energy

Stand in front of a mirror. Look yourself in the eye, smile at yourself, and say out loud:

- *I am moving into my positive YES energy.*
- *I am saying YES to this audience.*
- *I am ready to grow with this experience.*
- *I am now in my positive, open-minded, powerful YES energy.*

Repeat as needed and enjoy the power of YES!

Still not feeling high enough to get on stage? There's another way to elevate your spirits: Laughter.

Release Feel-Good Chemicals through Laughter

Laughter has a healing and relaxing effect. It reduces stress and eases tension. Laughing improves our mood; it makes us feel better about ourselves and the world around us. This is because our attitudes and gestures trigger certain chemical reactions in our body. Specifically, laughter produces endorphins and lowers stress hormones. Other benefits include muscle relaxation and pain relief, and it even improves our mental capacity. No joke!

Exercise 21: Laugh Your Heart Out!

No reason to laugh? You can easily find one. Try watching something funny online. Laughter decreases stress hormones and prompts the release of endorphins, which heighten your sense of well-being. It raises your oxytocin levels, and remember, oxytocin reduces your anxiety and makes you feel good about connecting with others.[17]

When I feel down and exhausted, I watch *Big Bang Theory*. It's the one show that never fails to make me laugh. It is such a relief to laugh, and we don't do it often enough. Laughter reduces stress, as it lowers the levels of stress hormones, such as cortisol and dopamine. Its relaxing effect positively impacts our health.[18]

Still nervous? Still no way to get those butterflies under control? The truth is that a certain level of nerves gives you an edge; it makes you seem vulnerable and, therefore, more likeable. But excessive jitters can make you freak out, stutter, or possibly even blank on stage, and they make it impossible to engage your audience in a way that serves your speaking goal.

Close your eyes for a moment and imagine one of the following: you're going to talk to a large audience tomorrow, you're presenting to a client, you're teaching a workshop, or you're hosting your own event. Feel into that visualization and notice what it feels like. Does it feel intimidating? Is there any speaking fear, any fear of rejection, any anxiety?

If your answer is, "yes," let's tap that fear away!

Exercise 22: Tap into Your Confidence and Courage
Tapping is a therapeutic treatment technique from Emotional Freedom Technique (EFT), which clears disruptions in your body's energy system and restores balance. It consists of lightly tapping on the end points of energy meridians in your body with two or three fingers of one or both hands and saying relevant statements out loud.

---

[17] James Altucher, "10 Unusual Ways to Release Oxytocin into Your Life," *Altucher Confidential*, accessed September 7, 2016, http://www.jamesaltucher.com/2012/08/10-unusual-ways-to-release-oxytocin-into-your-life/.
[18] Ibid.

Some typical tapping points are: top of head, eyebrow, side of eye, under eye, under nose, chin, and collarbone.

The following is a very simple form of tapping called opposite tapping, which can be applied without studying the details of EFT tapping. For now, all you need to know is that you lightly tap on the points listed below, while saying the corresponding statements out loud. It is important to feel into your statement, meaning you need to not only use your thoughts, but really feel into what you're saying so you feel the negative and then the positive impact. Alternate points after each statement as described below in parentheses.

You can always watch my YouTube video *Tap Through Your Fear and Step into Your Powerful Speaker Self,* or just follow the below instructions:

Start out by determining the level of your anxiety and giving it a number on a scale from 0 to 10, where 0 is no anxiety at all, and 10 is strong fear. Write that number down.

Opposite tapping: Say the statements in italics out loud while tapping.

- *I am nervous.* (Tap top of head – 1 hand.)
- *I am calm.* (Tap eyebrow – 1 hand on one side, or 2 hands on both sides.)

- *I am self-conscious.* (Tap side of eye – 1 hand on one side, or 2 hands on both sides.)
- *I am confident.* (Tap under eye– 1 hand on one side, or 2 hands on both sides.)
- *I am afraid.* (Tap under nose – 1 hand.)
- *I am fearless.* (Tap chin – 1 hand.)
- *I feel like a coward.* (Tap collarbone– 1 hand on one side, or 2 hands on both sides.)
- *I am courageous.* (Tap top of head.)
- *I feel little.* (Tap eyebrow.)
- *I feel big.* (Tap side of eye.)
- *I am jittery.* (Tap under eye.)
- *I am calm and serene.* (Tap under nose.)
- *I don't know how to calm my nerves.* (Tap chin.)
- *I know how to access a state of serenity.* (Tap collarbone.)
- *I feel powerless.* (Tap top of head.)
- *I know how to tap into my inner power. I am powerful.* (Tap eyebrow.)
- *I am scared.* (Tap side of eye.)
- *I am courageous.* (Tap under eye.)
- *I am nervous.* (Tap under nose.)
- *I am calm.* (Tap chin.)

Now observe whether the intensity of your fear has gone down. On a scale from 0 to 10, where is it now?

Repeat this tapping until your anxiety goes down below three, ideally to zero.

Chapter 9

LAST-MINUTE LIFE SAVERS

Y ou've made it to this moment... Awesome! There is very little time until your big moment. But wait! You are more tired than usual and you feel something is "off." You thought you were perfectly calm... until now. The truth is there are certain things we can't plan for. Even when we prepare carefully, last-minute nerves are not unusual. Here are some ways to deal with inner pandemonium.

Low-Energy Day? Doesn't Have to Be That Way!

We can't always plan our speaking gigs around our bio rhythm, moon phases, and occasional lows in our immune system, though we can certainly strengthen the latter with some simple practices that would fill an entire book by themselves.

It is key to eat lightly and drink plenty of water on the day of your gig. When I facilitate long workshops or on days when I don't feel 100% high energy, I have a set of items I like to use: Bergamot pure essential oil (naturally supports self-confidence) and a high-potency, natural energy booster. I only use energizing products made from natural, healthy ingredients, such as Vitamin B (specifically B12), monoatomic gold powder, chia seed drinks, guaraná, ginseng, and other energizing nutrients. These all help me enhance my mental focus on low-energy days and avoid getting drained during long sessions. They allow me to be vibrant and radiant throughout the entire event and completely connected to my positive YES energy

I also always carry some energy supplements in my bag when I go speak. Just knowing that I can fall back on them when needed has a huge psychological impact and gives me a sense of security. I absolutely have to know that I can rely on my memory, acuity, and a quick brain to process and act on opportunities that come up during my talk or seminar. This positively contributes to my serenity and confidence.

As always, whenever you experiment with a new product, check in with your medical caretaker, your physician or holistic practitioner. Again, I only recommend natural products without harmful side effects. Although my energy is high on most days, energy boosters are an essential item on my speaker's checklist, along with tech items and handouts. Download your free speaker's checklist at my website www.transformyourperformance.com.

Meeting and greeting people before the talk is another way to boost your energy before going on stage. It gives you a chance to not only make new friends, who then will be sitting in the audience as your supporters, but also to calm down your nerves as you realize that they are all human beings after all; they didn't come to fight you but to learn from you. While chatting with them, make sure you listen carefully so you can possibly pick up a few details that could come in handy as random comments during your talk. Referencing people makes them feel included and appreciated. Of course always use proper discernment as to what type of comments are appropriate for public mention.

From Jittery to Glittery
Who do you admire for their charisma, their inspiration, or their impact as a speaker, trainer, presenter or performer? Do you wish they'd pass you a portion of their charisma, their vigor or their unbridled enthusiasm as you step into your speaking situation? Check out the following exercise to find out how you can!

Exercise 23: Merge with Your Famous Role Model

See the role model of your choice in front of you, and ask them to stand behind you. Close your eyes and feel their energy surrounding you, embracing you. Imagine their courageous, charismatic, daring, and bold energy merging with your own energy. Allow that energy to support and inspire you at this time. True power multiplies as we share it with others, so there's no reason to feel guilty about accepting this generous power gift from them. You are not taking anything away from them; you are just being energetically inspired.

Soak in all this energetic power and inspiration. Feel the power in your body. When you feel this power energy intensely, confirm to yourself that you are now ready to face your audience, take a step forward, and imagine yourself stepping out of the merged position with your role model. Observe how much more confident you feel.

This exercise allows you to more powerfully and effectively tackle your upcoming challenge of finding yourself center stage, and with a little practice it can be done quickly and privately for some added confidence pre-speaking.

Get Present in Your Body

Dr. Albert Mehrabian conducted several studies on nonverbal communication.[19] He found that 7% of any message is conveyed through words, 38% through certain vocal elements, and 55% through nonverbal elements such as facial expressions, gestures, posture, etc. This means 93% of the information we receive about a person comes from non-verbal communication. Fifty-five percent of this non-verbal communication is attributed to body language and the rest to the quality of their voice.[20]

---

[19] Albert Mehrabian, "'Silent Messages'—A Wealth of Information About Nonverbal Communication (Body Language), *Albert Mehrabian*, accessed September 5, 2016, http://www.kaaj.com/psych/smorder.html.
[20] Ibid.

Think of your own experiences as a spectator. Was it the presenter's visual impression that you perceived first? Whether our first impression is positive or negative is determined by the way they show up: their outfit, their confidence, their facial expression, their energy, the way they walk onto the stage, and more.

This hypothesis is supported by research showing that the majority of people are visual learners, meaning that most people focus on and learn from what they see. They look at you, see you, and only then hear what you have to say (if they decide to still listen after what they saw). Voice is another important aspect, but I will leave that one to expert vocal coaches, which I am not. My forte is Body Consciousness, and that's what we will focus on here.

Let's face it, being fully present in your body and in your energy is key for a compelling, confident presence in speaking, in business, and in life! I don't know about you, but my body comes with me wherever I go, and so does my energy, whether I want that or not. We tend to forget that our bodies are always with us. Most of the time, we're not present in our bodies, which can be disempowering and lower other's perception of us, and with it our persuasiveness. This is why I came up with some exercises that help you get present in your body.

Exercise 24: Awaken Your Body

First, stand up and take a moment to feel your body and notice that you are a physical being. Start getting present in your body by making a fist and contracting your hands, fingers, and arms; hold this contraction for a few seconds, then relax both hands and arms. Now contract your shoulders: hold the tension there, then release all the tension in your shoulders. Move up to your neck, contract all your neck muscles; then relax this entire muscle group and release the tension in this area. Try isolating your head from your neck and contracting the muscles in your head only, then relax your head muscles and your scalp.

Now move back through your shoulders and into your chest; contract your chest, hold, and release. Do the same with your stomach and belly area and your gluteal muscles. Experiment with contracting and relaxing specific organs. Contract your thigh muscles; hold, and relax your thighs. Tense and release your calf muscles, and finally do the same for your feet and toes.

Notice how your body feels. Does it feel more awake, more alive? Do you feel more present in your body? This is a great first step leading into more Body Consciousness.

Body Consciousness
Your presence is a combination of your appearance, your inner power, and your Body Consciousness. And it's on purpose that I didn't say "body language," because what most people understand by body language is merely gestures, facial expressions, eye contact, etc. Your body language is only powerful when it's aligned with your personality and your energy, when it feels and looks authentic and natural. Body Consciousness is full awareness of your physical and energetic expression and your conscious use of both to enhance your impact. Note that this also includes your energy. It is an integral part of your body and of who you are.

Think about it, everything is energy. Who we are is energy. What we say, do, and think is energy. Yet, most of the time, we forget to pay attention to the quality of our energy and how to enhance our energetic impact. This is a shame because we can enhance our energetic impact very quickly. When we maximize our energetic impact, things start to shift. That's why I love teaching energy exercises in workshops and sharing them in this book.

Body Consciousness also means literally being conscious of your body–every single part of it! Take a moment and stroke your hand or forearm. Feel your skin. Then feel yourself inside your body. Close your eyes and pretend your eyes are turned inwards and you can actually look inside your skull. Then move your gaze down to your throat, all the way to your chest and into your shoulders and arms. Bring your inner attention to your chest. Breathe deeply. Feel the air filling your lungs and belly. Slowly come all the way down through your solar plexus, through your belly, your digestive tract, your abdomen, your reproductive organs, the base of your spine, and finally into your legs and feet. Imagine your blood flowing through your veins, your nerves attentive to causes for pain, your spine keeping you upright, your connective tissue holding everything together. There is much more going on in your body than would fit on this page, yet we hardly take the time to think about the miracle our body is and all the work it does for us every single minute. It may even feel strange to think about it.

When you're done with your inner body journey, wiggle your toes and fingers. Experience the fact that your body is an integral part of who you are. Giving your body the necessary positive attention enhances your presence as a speaker and as a leader.

Our body is always there for us. It comes with us wherever we go. We better pay attention to how we show up in our body and its energy, because doing so could make all the difference once you get in front of an audience.

If you want to increase your Body Consciousness over time, you can amplify your natural body language by having your presentations videotaped by a friend and reviewing them. Pay attention to what works to achieve the desired effect and interaction with your audience, and eliminate what's distracting. For example, you may want to create suspense or add humor or drama to parts of your speech with your gestures, movements, or facial expressions. Or you just want to express yourself and your message more intensely. After doing some of the exercises in this chapter, videotape yourself again, and notice the changes in your presence. Do you come across as more secure, more powerful, more engaging?

For today, stick with getting present in your body and energy, and see to it that your outfit, hair, and makeup are in great shape so you can make a compelling appearance at your event, making a strong first impression right from the moment you show up at your venue.

Are you ready for your event? If not, I have more tips and exercises for you coming up.

PART V:
DURING THE EVENT

This part is all about the gig itself: stepping into your power right before the event, making a captivating entry, and leaving a lasting impression. Here, I also share some sweet and short tools that help you stay focused and bring your calm back during your presentation or meeting, if it becomes necessary.

Chapter 10

GET READY TO TAKE CENTER STAGE

reviously, I introduced you to the Tap into Your Power exercise. The following is a shortcut, a shorter version of that same exercise, which instantly helps you plug in your inner power cord when you only have a few seconds left before you bravely walk into a room or onto a stage:

Exercise 25: Plug into Your Power Shortcut

Place a hand on your solar plexus area and take a moment to feel your very own personal power! What you focus on, expands. Breathe into this area and simply allow your inner power to expand and trust that it will!

This is a fast and effective tool to control your stage fright and sharpen your focus. It's the one thing I use every single time before stepping into a speaking or otherwise challenging situation. While I play with variations of other techniques, this exercise always stays with me.

Remember, managing your jitters is not the only purpose of this tool. When you tap into your inner power, those around you will see it in your outer presence. When you prepare physically and energetically for your meeting or event your inner magnet is activated, and you can draw your audience in before you even say a single word.

Breathe

Another simple way of captivating your audience is a deep breath after making your appearance on stage and acknowledging the host, just before you kick off your talk. Most people expect you to talk right away, so a moment of silence often comes as a surprise, and surprises call attention.

That's why the first thing you want to do is take a breath, slowly and deeply. It doesn't only calm your nervous system and allows you to focus better by sending more oxygen to your brain cells. It raises your ability to deliver your presentation with serenity and awareness. Depending on the size and set-up of the room, a deep breath is often all it takes to bring the entire group together, to draw them all in. Having the guts to just stand there and breathe without talking generates respect and curiosity. Often it is the first step to commanding the room.

Send Good Wishes

As you step in front of a room, energetically connect with your audience and send them good wishes. They may not be able to receive your good wishes on a conscious level, but their subconscious will pick them up, and their friendliness towards you will increase.

Be Prepared for Any Audience

Not too long ago, I thought I was over the risk of getting thrown off by that one person in the audience that you know wants to see only your worst. You know who I'm talking about: that person who is driven by envy, jealousy, or just a tremendous need to compete with you for some reason. It turns out I wasn't over that risk just a few short months ago, and I was thrown *way* off by that one person in the audience.

After a highly successful day I went to a networking event, which included a pitch from the front of the room. When it was my turn to grab the mic, I felt pretty good, and I started out really well. All of a sudden, the negative energy from this woman near the front of the room threw me off base. I hesitated and I didn't know what to say next. We only had 30 seconds, and here I was hesitating and tongue-tied. My pitch didn't come out right, and the result was an awkward pause. When I was timed out by the organizers' assistant, I just stood there in disbelief and stared at him instead of gracefully wrapping it up. I felt like crap. Ever been there?

Somehow my subconscious gave that person in the audience power over me, without me even noticing. As someone who knows how sensitive I am to other people's energies, I hadn't braced myself energetically, and the results were terrible. I felt like a failure.

Exercise 26: That One Person in the Audience

Here's a simple exercise to brace yourself when you see "that one person" in the audience that clearly doesn't want you to succeed.

First of all, declare that it's their problem to feel envious or jealous; it's not your problem. Then release yourself from the obligation to respond to their negative energy. Often times we respond to negativity because we feel it needs or deserves a response. This isn't true. You can ignore it completely. At the same time as you free yourself from this obligation to respond, free that person in the audience from the "obligation" to negatively impact you. Finally, imagine a bubble of white or golden light surrounding you and protecting you. Feel the power in this ball of energy. Everything is energy. Protection is energy, and energy is protection.

Practice this exercise slowly in a safe place first; take your time. Repeat the exercise until you feel like you can do this in a matter of a few seconds. I suggest you memorize the steps to follow so you can do them quickly and effortlessly when needed.

People who have used this simple technique in situations of serious threat have been able to avert the risk; some have reported entire groups of dangerous possible attackers walking away from them in the street when they used this technique. I applied it often late at night in Brazil when walking home from the bus stop didn't feel completely safe. This simple technique would have kept me from having such an unpleasant experience at that networking event. Next time I will remember to practice and be prepared!

In the next section, I will share some practices that can make your presentation or talk more engaging, effective, and memorable. At the same time, you will find that speaking in public thus becomes a more satisfying experience for yourself, which you will want to repeat over and over again.

Chapter 11

Awe Your Audience

Your big moment is here. You have made it all the way to the most exhilarating portion! This is where the real fun begins. Stay connected to the guiding light of your mission and vision and connect back to it whenever you have a moment of insecurity. I have found myself interpreting a serious look on a listener's face for criticism or doubt, when in fact it turned out they were among my greatest fans. Instead of premature assumptions about your audience's thoughts, stay focused on your message, on engaging the audience, and just doing your best. Here are some tips and tricks to support a dynamic and impactful performance and awe your audience.

Look the Tiger in the Eye

Another trick to use when on stage is to make eye contact. Look someone in the eye. When you make a personal connection with one individual, this reduces your anxiety because rather than drawing a line between yourself and an anonymous audience, you are establishing a connection with a specific human being.

Have a Blast

It's crucial that you have a good time while you speak. If you are not passionate about your topic, how can you expect to captivate your audience? When you are well-prepared, your content is solid, and you want to make a difference, it becomes easy to have a blast, and it will be contagious. Relax. Sharing your message is fun!

Engage Your Audience

Have you ever witnessed a talk where the speaker only presented facts? It's not that exciting, unless the facts are surprising enough by themselves. However, your talk becomes more engaging when your audience is actively included in the presentation.

Interactive talks are my favorite. As a listener, they help me get the most out of a given topic. As a speaker, they help me hook my audience, keep their attention high, and make them feel heard and acknowledged. After all, I want them to get the most value out of the time they spend with me.

It can be challenging to pay attention to a speaker. Sitting in a chair for an extended length of time can be boring and make us want to disengage. However, when we have an active role in what's happening around us, whether it's in the form of a group or partner exercise, a visualization exercise, or some physical or energetic activity, we suddenly become interested, engaged and invested in what we're hearing and learning. The same is true for your audience during your presentation. Engage them. Do anything that converts passive listeners into active participants. This can be done by asking questions that require them to come up with an answer or even write their answer down. You may ask individuals to reply to the entire group at a mic or silently in their minds. What works best will depend on the size of the audience, the set-up of the space, and the subject matter of your speech or presentation.

Involving your audience in the conversation makes your talk not only more engaging but also more dynamic and memorable. It helps them remember important details more easily and vividly. Having your audience actively participate acknowledges their presence in the room and their importance. They become players in your game, and the two of you connect on a deeper level. Most importantly, when you offer them exercises with a practical application of your theoretical content, they see the true value of what you came to share, which is key when you intend to sell your services or products.

At times, engaging your audience can best be achieved through group work. Depending on the event type and size, I have the attendees pair up or work in small groups. I encourage them to partner with people they don't know so they can learn new perspectives they may not be exposed to within their normal circle of friends. Group work connects. It is a wonderful bonding tool, and most people will welcome this opportunity to network. This also gives the more introverted attendees a possibility to voice their point of view without having to get up and speak to the entire room. Set a timer so you don't have to watch the time during the entire exercise.

There's a nice side effect of group exercises; they give you a breathing break during which you can glance over your notes and make sure you have covered all the important points of a certain topic. Make sure to check in with the room from time to time to see whether any group needs further instructions or support.

At the end of the group work, you may want to give several people, or one representative per team, a chance to share their findings or observations in public. This is a fabulous way to spark a lively discussion. Just make sure you're still in control as the moderator so you stay within your topic and timeframe. You also want to see to it that the general direction of the discussion covers content that's relevant to most people in the room. If anyone touches on a very narrow issue that only refers to their specific situation, offer to take it offline and move on with your talk. This is a great way to continue a conversation with someone who may become your client as a result of a follow-up call.

Share Your Spotlight to Amplify It
Another way to keep your audience's mind from drifting is to ask questions and have them talk about their own experiences. It makes them feel important and listened to. The best moment to give your audience a chance to share their aha's is after breaks or towards the

end of your talk, presentation, or session. Providing an opportunity to voice their learnings is a way to obtain immediate social proof and evidence of the validity and value of your work. If you're speaking to a large room and have a mic, definitely have them use it. Some participants will love this chance to be in the spotlight.

Never underestimate this portion of your presentation or talk! It makes for great testimonials, and when people share their enthusiasm and fervor, it spreads to other people in the room and kindles their fire as well. That positive energy is good! Last, but not least, they will learn from each other and you from them.

PART VI:
AFTER THE EVENT

The event is not over when you walk off stage or leave a meeting. Often times we are so relieved that our speaking gig or presentation is behind us that we forget about all the important post-event activities, which help us grow as speakers and increase our success. This part is a quick reminder for you to schedule time for these critical activities.

Chapter 12

DEBRIEF, FOLLOW UP AND CELEBRATE!

Learn from the Experience

Every single speaking experience is an opportunity to "up" your learning curve. On the day of the event or the day after, set apart some time to reflect on what went well and what you can improve going forward. Keep a journal, or an electronic file, where you document these thoughts, and include ideas and suggestions to enhance your content, persuasiveness, and impact in the future.

If there was a trusted friend among the audience, schedule a debrief. Be sure to listen to their feedback carefully without getting defensive, and make notes. Add their feedback to your journal.

The Power Is in the Follow-up

You will find the power (and the money) is in the follow-up. If you were a guest speaker and were not offered the opportunity to contact every single person in the audience, look for ways to send a "thank you" note through the host. Maybe include a link to a relevant article or some other information that leads them to your website www.transformyourperformance.com and invite them to sign up for your mailing list, if they haven't already. Also remember to thank your host for the opportunity. A hand-written card gives an extra personal touch.

If you asked the participants during the event to sign up for your mailing list in exchange for a free product (like a checklist, an e-book, or a video), input their contact information as soon as possible and get their gift out to them right away. If you offered free consultations, make them happen as soon as possible. Ideally, you already scheduled them at the event.

In the case of client presentations, whether in the name of your employer or your own company, follow up with an email that includes a re-cap and next steps.

There are many ways to follow up. Be creative and keep a list of your options as you discover the best ones for your specific situations over time.

Celebrate

When you have worked up the courage to get in front of an audience and expose yourself, it's time to celebrate. You did it! Take a moment to be proud of yourself. Every single time you present is a move forward, whether you sold something or not. The only way you'll get better and more experienced as a speaker is to go out and do it, so celebrate every time you do so! Every single gig is an opportunity to learn and practice, and most importantly, to be heard and seen and acknowledge yourself as a speaker. It's an item to add to your speaker's sheet, and it's a step towards getting paid as a speaker if that's a goal you are pursuing.

Chapter 13

CONCLUDING THOUGHTS

Whether you are a new speaker or whether you have a long list of speaking experiences under your belt, I hope the exercises you learned and applied helped you make your event more gratifying. Add them to your speaker's toolbox, make them a part of your routine, and think about other challenging business (or personal) situations where they may be useful to you. If you found value in the exercises, please invite others to learn them and read this book. I want you to get a kick out of speaking, just as I do now.

It's show time! Grab a mic! It's time to shine your brilliance out to the world. You got this!

If you feel like some extra support could make it easier for you to take the stage, or if you just want a little push so you can move to the next level in your career as a leader or a thought leader, contact me through my website www.transformyourperformance.com to set up a call. I'd be delighted to learn more about your mission and your vision.

Leaders and speakers like you who have an important message to share are needed in the world. That's why I want you to come out of your hiding place and speak up, stand out and shine.

YOUR MESSAGE MATTERS

Can't wait to read about your success stories. They mean a lot to me. As you reap results with the techniques in this book, email me at regina@transformyourperformance.com.
To your brilliance and success!

ABOUT THE AUTHOR

Regina Huber is a Transformational Leadership Coach, CEO & Founder of TRANSFORM YOUR PERFORMANCE (www.transformyourperformance.com), a Speaker with a Passion for Dance, and a Diversity Advocate. With her signature *Powerful Leadership Transformation (PLT)* system she shows her clients how to step into their role as leaders with an empowering mindset, distinctive uniqueness, a body-conscious presence, and as a result, effective action. As powerful leaders, they can make a bigger impact and create more wealth for clients, companies, themselves and the causes they want to support.

Regina grew up in Germany, speaks 5 languages and has over 18 years of international experience in the corporate business world in six countries, including management positions at The Boston Consulting Group in Europe, Latin America, and the U.S. Before moving to New York City, she owned businesses in Argentina and Brazil. She has studied a variety of the most advanced holistic healing techniques. Her big love is dance, which has made her an expert in body-conscious presence. She translated 12 books, most of which on Argentine Tango.

Regina offers customized coaching programs and group workshops based on her system *Powerful Leadership Transformation (PLT)*. She also offers workshops focusing specifically on female leadership to drive gender parity in leadership. Regina is available as a keynote speaker for events and conferences. To find out more about Regina and *Powerful Leadership Transformation (PLT)*, check out her website www.transformyourperformance.com.